HEARINGS

BY THE

BOARD OF ALDERMEN. OF BOSTON

ON THE

Petition of the Citizens' Gas Light Co.

NOV. 9, 16, 30, and DEC. 7, 1874.

PHONOGRAPHICALLY REPORTED BY J. M. W. YERRINTON.

BOSTON:
PRINTED BY RAND, AVERY, AND COMPANY.
1874.

I.

HEARING

BY THE BOARD OF ALDERMEN OF BOSTON

ON THE

PETITION OF CITIZENS' GAS LIGHT CO.,

NOV. 9, 1874.

TESTIMONY OF

Geo. O. Carpenter	5
Geo. P. Baldwin	17
Leopold Morse	34
John P. Kennedy	37
W. W. Greenough	55
Opening Argument of R. M. Morse, Jun.	129
John C. Pratt	139
Geo. B. Neal	146
W. W. Greenough	167

ARGUMENTS.

Mr. Field's	207
Mr. Putnam's	214
Mr. Morse's	218
Mr. Hyde's	228

HEARING NOVEMBER 9.

TESTIMONY OF GEORGE O. CARPENTER.

MR. CHAIRMAN, AND GENTLEMEN OF THE BOARD.

THE counsel (P. A. Collins, Esq.) has stated pretty much all that I could say, except, that in behalf of my associates, I desire to say, that we come here purely in a business matter, believing that the supply of gas to the city of Boston is of so great moment that it should not be in the hands of a great monopoly, as it now exists. You are well aware that the Boston Gas Light Company has held the control of the supply of gas to the citizens of Boston now for nearly half a century; that they have no particular restrictions. I believe they are under the care of your board, as are all corporations; but so far as price is concerned, I take it, they can charge whatever in their judgment they see fit, and you and I and all the other citizens must bow assent. Now, as a citizen of Boston, I believe that it is the right of the citizens of Boston to have an honorable, fair, and healthy competition in the matter of the supply of gas, and this company has been organized with perfectly honest intentions, by men who desire to do business, with an absolute capital to the extent of over a million of dollars already in hand, ready to be used whenever we desire. With these ideas, we request from you the privilege of erecting works and laying pipes to compete with the Boston Gas Light Company. As I look at it, as an individual and as a citizen of Boston, I naturally see that if such a privilege is granted us, and we are allowed to become a company, and to lay our pipes, one of the first things will be a reduction in the price of gas supplied by the Boston Gas Light Company; and I ask you, as intelligent citizens of Boston, if a reduction of price, no matter how little it may be, suppose it is fifty cents per thousand feet, does not benefit every consumer of gas in the city of Boston? If their receipts are more than a million and a half dollars annually, and they reduce the price from $2.50 to $2.00 per thousand, are not $300,000 saved to the consumers of gas in the city of Boston? Without being able to state positively, I believe that, at the present time, an experiment, which is a very fortunate one for the citizens of Detroit, is being tried in that city, a new gas company having been allowed to come in competition with the old one, whereby the present price is one dollar per thousand feet; possibly that may not remain long, being too low; but such is the effect of the competition, and certainly the citizens of Detroit are benefited by the means.

I do not desire, Mr. Chairman and Gentlemen of the Board, to take up your time. I simply wish to confirm what has been said by the counsel as to the principles on which we are intending to do business. We shall be glad to have you restrict us in every way that brain or legal talent can possibly devise, by which the great bugbear — which I know exists, because I have heard it referred to so often; namely, that if we get this charter we shall sell out to the old company — shall be laid.

Now, Mr. Chairman and Gentlemen of the Board, you may put any restriction upon us which you see fit. I am very well aware that it is impossible for you to go to the extent of restricting parties who own the stock from selling it; but you can provide, that we shall forfeit our charter, if we undertake to sell out as a company; or, if it be possible or legal, you may require any amount to be deposited, which shall be forfeited if we do not do a strictly honorable and straightforward competing business. We shall be very glad to have you put upon us any restriction which you think proper. We have come before you honestly, and intend to do just what our petition sets forth.

MR. COLLINS: I will ask you, Mr. Carpenter, if your

idea is embraced in section fourth of the bill presented to the Legislature?

A. Most cheerfully I will agree to any thing of that kind.

Q. You proposed that in the Legislature?

A. I did, sir.

MR. COLLINS: We have a number of gentlemen here, but Mr. Carpenter has stated our case. He has stated what the other corporators will state, and it will be but a repetition, it seems to me, to introduce other witnesses to the same point. Mr. Leopold Morse, Mr. Henry Smith, Dr. Thayer, and other corporators are here, and will answer any questions that may be put to them. We reserve, of course, the right to rebut any evidence that may be presented against granting this charter.

THE CHAIRMAN: Are there any other persons present desiring to be heard in favor of or in opposition to the granting of this petition?

R. M. MORSE, JR., ESQ.: The Boston Gas Light Co. appears here and desires to be heard, but, before making any statement, we should like the privilege of putting some interrogatories to some of the gentlemen who are produced here by the petitioners. I should like to ask Mr. Carpenter some questions.

MR. COLLINS: That is exactly what we want.

Q. (By MR. MORSE). When was this company formed?

A. I can not give you the date; it is on the paper you hold in your hand.

Q. The date of the charter is the 19th of October last?

A. Yes, sir.

Q. When were the articles of association subscribed?

A. My impression is on the day before or on that day.

Q. How much money has been paid in?

A. Five thousand dollars.

Q. Have you made any arrangements for building the works?

A. No, sir. It was not considered practicable for us to do that. Our company being formed solely with the object of supplying gas to the city of Boston, it was not considered prudent that we should make any further arrangements than to first come here with our petition.

Q. Have you decided what to make the gas out of?

A. Out of coal, sir, unless modern appliances shall be shown to be better. I know nothing better than coal.

Q. You don't propose to make it from petroleum?

A. No, sir.

Q. Or from Naphtha?

A. No sir; or any thing but coal.

Q. The same kind of coal used by the Boston Gas Light Co.?

A. I am not equal to answering that, sir; but fortunately there are gentlemen here that can answer such questions, and to whom we should be very glad to have you put such questions.

Q. From what kind of coal do you propose to manufacture your gas?

A. I don't pretend to know anything of the kinds of coal. I simply answer the question, that we propose to make it out of coal, and only coal. Beyond that, I can give you no further answer.

Q. Have you made any estimate of the cost of manufacturing gas from coal?

A. I have not made any estimate.

Q. You are not personally acquainted with it?

A. I do not pretend to come here as being a proficient, at all, in the art of gas making.

Q. Has any statement been submitted to your company of the cost of manufacturing gas?

A. We have had general ideas, because this matter has been for a long time under discussion; and at our meetings last winter, when we were before the Legislature, and since, we have been actively at work in getting such information as we could; and general statements have been submitted to us by very intelligent people ; and such statements have allowed us to feel, that it was certainly, at the price the Boston Gas Light Co. are now charging, a very fair business to carry on.

Q. Who has made the general statements you refer to?

A. Various gentlemen that we have talked with from time to time.

Q. What ones, sir?

A. Well, I don't know that I can give you any particular ones. Mr. Kennedy is one.

Q. What Mr. Kennedy?

A. Mr. Kennedy of New-York City. He is a gas engineer, and is present.

Q. The one connected with the New-York Mutual?

A. The one connected with the New-York Mutual.

Q. Any one else?

A. I am not familiar with the matter, and should not be able to answer the question.

Q. Of course I do not ask you for any thing you do not know yourself; but do you know of anybody else who has given your company " general ideas," as you say ?

A. No, sir. I cannot say that I have any thing more than the general idea I have obtained from talking with directors of gas companies. I am interested in one myself in a suburban town, and have talked frequently with the officers of that company.

Q. Now, what are the "general ideas" which you or the company have on this subject?

A. Our general ideas are primarily these: that there should be, with the great growth of this city of Boston, an opposition company for the protection of its citizens. That is the primary reason for our entering into this matter, believing that it is for the benefit of all concerned, and that the city, as it grows in size, will only need more and more this competition for the good of its citizens.

Q. Then, without reference to the question of the exact cost, you would, on general principles, have every street dug up, and two sets of gas-pipes laid down through them?

A. If I thought I could gain for the citizens of Boston the advantages that I believe can be gained from having another company, I would feel that the very temporary inconvenience (being done by slow and sure degrees) that would be occasioned by taking up the streets should be encountered for the sake of carrying out the idea?

Q. Have you looked into the matter of the cost of making gas by the Boston Gas Light Co., so as to satisfy yourself as to whether the price is higher than it ought to be?

A. No, sir. As I said before, I am not a proficient in gas making. I should have to refer you to those who know much more about it than myself.

Q. Your general idea is, that competition is a good thing?

A. That is the main idea upon which we enter this field.

Q. Have you considered how much capital it would take to build gas works and lay pipes through the streets of the city?

A. We have considered that in a general way, and have felt, as a matter of course, that the amount of capital we are about to ask for, which is a million dollars — our charter providing for a million dollars. . . . .

Q. What do you mean by your charter providing for a million dollars?

A. I mean to say, the by-laws of our company. I mean to say, that a million of dollars would not begin to give us the amount of money we desire.

Q. Have you already subscriptions to the amount of a million of dollars?

A. We have, sir.

Q. Where is that paper?

A. It is where we can produce it at the proper time.

Q. Have you any objection to producing it?

A. Yes, sir, I have. I don't think it is proper to produce a private document for the opposite side to read. I am very willing to show it to a committee of the Board of Aldermen at the proper time.

Q. I was going to ask, if you had any objection to the Board of Aldermen seeing it?

A. Not in the least. It must come before them at the proper time, I suppose.

Q. What do you allow for the cost of the works?

A. I cannot tell you. I cannot answer any of the practical questions relating to the manufacture of gas.

Q. Do you know whether a million of dollars would be sufficient to build the works and lay the pipes?

A. My judgment would be, that it would be very far below the amount that would be necessary.

Q. What do you propose to do, then?

A. We propose to do as any other company under ordinary circumstances would do — to do the next best thing. If we must go to the Legislature and get an increase of capital, we shall certainly do it.

Q. Do you expect to start any operations before you go to the Legislature for an increase of capital?

A. Yes, sir.

Q. What do you expect to do before you go to the Legislature?

A. We expect at once to make the proper arrangements for making gas to supply the city of Boston.

Q. I will ask you if the Board of Aldermen should tonight authorize you to take up the principal streets of the city of Boston, what should you do?

A. We should not undertake to touch any of them for the next year.

Q. Then the Aldermen for next year would do as well, wouldn't they?

A. We will see when next year comes.

Q. You propose to go to the Legislature next winter?

A. We have not laid out any plan for the next winter.

We are simply here now in a business way to ask this permission, and having obtained it, believing it is right and proper, one of the next things we should naturally do would be to look about and secure a location upon which to erect our works.

Q. (By GEORGE PUTNAM, ESQ., *Counsel for the South Boston Gas Company.*) Have you made up your mind where you shall begin these works?

A. No, sir.

Q. Do you intend to confine yourself to any particular part of the city, or do you wish to have leave to take up the streets in all parts of the city, including the suburbs and newly annexed portions.

A. We wish properly to compete with the other company, as far as we can. We expect to act always, I may say, under the direction of the Board of Aldermen.

Q. But do you expect, or do you intend to go on and lay pipes in all parts of the city, or are you willing to confine yourselves to any particular localities?

A. We ask to do whatever the Boston Gas Light Company do, or whatever the Boston Gas Light Company are allowed to do; because we want to be in competition with them.

Q. Do you desire, or do you ask to go outside the limits now occupied by the Boston Gas Light Company?

A. No, sir, we do not; for, if I understood Mr. Greenough before the Legislature, correctly, he can go to the western end of Massachusetts.

Q. Perhaps you do not quite understand my question. I ask you if you propose to go beyond the limits of the Boston Gas Light Company?

A. If they cover the territory of Boston, I should not.

Q. Then you wish to be at liberty to go all over the whole territory of Boston?

A. We wish to go wherever they go.

Q. I will put the specific question: Do you wish to go to South Boston?

A. We have not thought of the matter of localities. We have not thought of the new districts. The matter has not come up at all.

Q. Then you have not made up your mind at all where you shall begin to lay your pipes if you get this permission.

A. No, sir, we have not. We should propose always to act under the direction of the Board of Aldermen.

Q. You desire, however, as I understand, a general permission from the Board of Aldermen, to go any where you choose in the city of Boston?

A. Yes, sir; that is the way our petition reads, I believe.

Q. I understand you to say that you have not made any very close estimate of what it would cost you to make gas, or what your works would cost you?

A. No, sir, I have not. You ask me individually?

Q. Certainly, sir. I am questioning you wholly as an individual. I do not know that you appear here in any other capacity. I believe you have not satisfied yourself of the exact amount of profit that is made by the other companies which now occupy this territory, have you?

A. No, sir, only in a general way. I can see the great growth and prosperity of the Boston Gas Light Company without much figuring.

Q. You have a general impression, then, that these other gas companies make a great deal of money, and if you can get permission to build works along side of them, covering the same ground and competing with them, you must be able to make money. Is that it?

A. Certainly, as a business man I would not go into the operation if I thought I was going to lose money.

Q. Are you willing to state what your own subscription to this million dollars is?

A. I can say, that for myself and my associates, I am at liberty to pay in $250,000.

Q. And that subscription you have made and are ready

to pay in, without any further investigation as to the profit you can make out of it, or what your chances of loss will be, than you have testified to here?

A. Not any more than myself and associates have made; but for myself, I should not desire any thing more.

Q. On whose judgment are you and your associates ready to pay $250,000 into a business of which you know no more than you have stated here?

A. I should not feel clear to make a direct answer to that question, because I should not care to name the parties from whom I have received, or know I can receive, funds.

Q. Then I understand you that you are not willing to state the party on whose judgment you propose, for yourself and others, to make this large subscription?

A. I do not think I should say it was on any one's judgment, but on an idea. We all have a general idea, starting from the fact of the Boston Gas Light Company's commencing with $75,000 capital, and of its having to-day several millions of property that it has made, in addition to its dividends, all of which, in our opinion, has come out of the people.

Q. Well, Mr. Carpenter, do you mean to say that you are ready to put $250,000, for yourself and others, into a business of which you know nothing, except that somebody else has made money in it, in precisely the same locality in which you propose to go into competition?

A. No, sir. I don't say that I propose to do that for myself; I do say, for myself and associates.

Q. You are ready to put $250,000 into competition with the Boston Gas Light Company, without having made any further investigation of the sources of profit, or the chances of loss, than you have stated here to-night?

A. I do not think I can have stated a great many of the details of the conversations that we have had on the subject; and various things have tended to cause me to make up my mind, and very much fuller information may have tended to make up my associates' minds.

Q. I understood you to say that you went into this enterprise on general ideas?

A. It is general. I can make up my mind to-day on general points as I meet them.

Q. Did you ever make up your mind before to put $250,000 into any company on general ideas?

A. No, sir, I am sorry to say I never had $250,000 that I could put into any operation.

Q. Then, for yourself and others?

A. For myself and others I never had occasion to invest that amount of money until the present time.

Q. I understood you to decline to state who these associates are for whom you are putting in $250,000?

A. I prefer not to state them now, as there will be another hearing, and as we may have a better opportunity to take up the matter, I should prefer not to place them in that position.

Q. Are you willing to state what proportion of that subscription is on your own individual account?

A. Well, I do not know that I have any particular hesitancy in saying that I should be a stockholder to the extent of from three to five thousand dollars.

Q. From three to five thousand dollars, then, is the extent of your money subscription?

A. Of my own; yes, sir.

Q. That is a cash subscription?

A. Yes, sir; I know of no other.

Q. Then it is only from three to five thousand dollars that you propose to invest in this company?

A. I do not know that.

Q. That you at present propose to invest?

A. I have not yet matured my plans. I have not yet settled down on what I might take, and what some one else might take.

Q. But I understand you that five thousand dollars is the outside of what you will probably take?

A. I say what I will probably take. I want to give you

an answer, because you seem to want to press that point; but I may not take a fifth, or a tenth, and my associates may not take half that amount; that of course would depend—

Q. Let us see if we understand each other. I understood you to say, that for yourself and associates, you had made a subscription of two hundred and fifty thousand dollars, and I understood you afterwards to say that your own share in that subscription would probably be from three to five thousand dollars; that is your statement as you wish to leave it, is it?

A. Yes, sir.

Q. I understood you to say that five thousand dollars had been paid in?

A. Yes, sir.

Q. What was your share of that?

A. Five hundred.

Q. Are you willing to state what suburban company you are connected with?

A. I am a stockholder in the Wakefield Gas Co.

Q. Have the profits of that company been so excessive that you are induced to embark in this new enterprise?

A. The profits have been very fair indeed. I have no cause of complaint.

Q. Should you be willing to start a competing company there?

A. Not under the present state of things; but in due process of time we may arrive at that point.

Q. Do you think that, if a competing gas-light company were started in Wakefield, with duplicate works, duplicate pipes, and every thing, the citizens of Wakefield would get their gas cheaper for the next quarter of a century, say, than they would if the present company alone occupied the ground?

A. Do you think that is a fair comparison?

Q. I do not put it as a comparison: I put it as a question.

A. I do not think Wakefield is in any better position to have a duplicate company to-day than the Boston Gas-Light Company was in the days of George Darracott.

Q. Well, you do not think it would be a good thing to duplicate the gas company in Wakefield?

A. I do not think it would pay at the present time.

Q. My question was not whether it would pay, but whether you thought the people would get their gas cheaper, for the next twenty years, with the two gas companies competing there?

A. With so sparsely a settled population, I should hardly say they would.

Q. But a sparsely-settled population would be just as much benefited by competition as a dense population?

A. As I said before, I do not think the two places are to be compared at all.

Q. I do not make any comparison: I simply ask you the question.

A. I think, then, I must answer, that competition everywhere is healthy; but I can conceive also that a business may be overdone; and I should say that to put two gas companies into Wakefield would be a good deal like overdoing the business. Two gas companies in Boston would hardly come under that head.

Q. Now, do you think two gas companies in Boston could furnish gas to the citizens cheaper than one company could?

A. I think they would.

TESTIMONY OF GEORGE P. BALDWIN.

Q. (By Mr. Hyde.) Are you one of the proposed incorporators here?

A. I am.

Q. Are you acting in good faith?

A. I think I am.

Q. Are you proposing to put your own money into the company, if the privilege is granted to build works and lay pipes in the streets?

A. I am, to the last dollar I am worth; and to stand behind it and furnish the citizens of Boston with gas.

Q. You propose to put your money in in good faith?

A. Every dollar I have, and all I can borrow.

Q. You are willing to put your money in, and take the risk of being able to furnish the citizens of Boston with better and cheaper gas than they now have?

A. I am.

Q. And if you don't do it, it is your loss and not the citizens'?

A. It is.

Q. Are you one of the directors of the public institutions?

A. I am.

Q. Do you manufacture your gas there?

A. We do.

Q. From what?

A. Coal.

Q. What does it cost, or what has it cost, since you have been there, per thousand feet?

A. I can't give you the exact figures; but I can give you, within four or five cents per thousand, the average cost since I have been a director on that Board. It cost at the House of Correction and Deer Island, $1.05 per thousand.

Q. Is there any other public institution where it is made?

A. It is made in the Lunatic Hospital, House of Correction, the House of Industry, and the Home for the Poor.

Q. You say it costs $1.05 per thousand feet?

A. Yes, sir.

Q. What does the Boston Gas Light Co. now charge the citizens?

A. They charge $2.50 per thousand feet.

Q. With that margin, you are willing, as one, to put in your money and build works to supply the citizens, if you can have the privilege of doing so?

A. Yes, sir.

Cross-Examination.

Q. (By Mr. Morse.) Who has charge of the manufacture of this gas at Deer Island?

A. We have a regular engineer employed. I don't know his name, but I can ascertain.

Q. Is the gas made in more than one institution?

A. It is made at the House of Industry at Deer Island, and at the House of Correction at South Boston.

Q. Who has charge of it at the House of Industry?

A. The House of Industry is under the charge of a general superintendent; but he employs under him, of course, an engineer. The name of the engineer I don't know.

Q. Is that the engineer who has charge of making the gas?

A. I think it is, although I won't say unqualifiedly that it is, from the fact that I have never met those particular employees; but I have the report each month before me, as well as my associates, and know that what I state as to the cost is correct.

Q. Is there a report kept of the cost of gas?

A. Yes, sir.

Q. Where is that record?

A. That record is in the hands of the superintendent, or superintendent's clerk, up to the time it is made, and then it goes into the hands of the Board of Directors of Public Institutions.

Q. Where may it be found?

A. I think you may find it at their office in Pemberton Square, which is very near here.

Q. Does that show also the cost of manufacture at the House of Correction?

A. Yes, sir; that is, I think there are two. I don't know whether the items are given in regard to each one, or whether the two establishments are aggregated, but I know what I state is correct, as far as I can remember. What I state is within a few cents, more or less.

Q. What are the items of cost which you include?

A. The items of cost, of course, do not concern laying the pipes, do not concern the works. They concern simply the cost of manufacturing the gas out of coal at that island.

Q. What do you include in the cost of manufacturing gas from coal, — what are the items you include?

A. The expense, as I understand, does not include interest on laying pipes, or the cost of whatever works they have erected.

Q. Is labor included?

A. Well, I suppposse it may be. I don't know what they calculate their labor to be worth.

Q. Do you know whether it is included or not?

A. I suppose that labor at the island is merely a nominal sum.

Q. Then when you state the cost of gas at these institutions, you don't allow any thing for labor?

A. I do, sir, for we are obliged to employ a competent supervisor or superintendent for its manufacture.

Q. Well, take the ordinary labor, the ordinary manual labor,—isn't that performed by the prisoners confined there?

A. Undoubtedly; the carrying the coal in wheelbarrows, and the ordinary labor of that kind, would be performed, of course, by the labor there; but, on the other hand, we, of course, work against great odds in manufacturing gas at such a point as that, over what a company like the Boston Gas Co., or the South Boston Gas Co., or other companies, would work.

Q. Without going into that quite yet, let me ask you a question or two more about the labor. How many laborers did you allow for in making this estimate of the cost at the House of Industry?

A. The only labor which is allowed for in the estimate of the cost is simply the labor which is paid for.

Q. How much is that?

A. That question I can't answer definitely, although I suppose the cost of labor per cubic foot in the manufacture of gas is an indifferent item when you come to sum up the total cost. The principal cost, if I understand it correctly, and I have no doubt I am correct, is the material itself which the gas is made from.

Q. Yes: but still you hardly answer my question, — what amount is allowed for labor in those institutions?

A. I answer the question as carefully as I am capable of. I simply say to you, that the ordinary labor, what would be called coarse labor, is done by the inmates of the institution.

Q. You don't know, as I understand you, how much ought to be allowed if that had to be paid for?

A. I can't tell you exactly.

Q. Now, in regard to the coal, what kinds of coal are used?

A. I think I could tell pretty nearly how much labor is employed in the manufacture of gas. I think each of these reports, which are brought up from the Island, gives the number of days' labor; and if it would be any advantage to you, and I presume it would, and certainly I think it would be to the Aldermen, to know, I should be very glad to have those reports brought here, and I will endeavor to have them laid before you.

Q. What kinds of coal are used at the House of Industry?

A. A coal is used there from which a product is produced which, according to my eyes, if they reflect correctly, is much better than the light in the City Hall.

Q. That hardly answers my question as to what kind of coal is used?

A. I think what is termed bituminous coal.

Q. Hasn't it some other name, — some special name?

A. I can't quite remember. I have heard it said that they use the best coal; that they consider the best coal the cheapest coal which they can use, and my impression is that it is coal which costs, when anthracite coal is six dollars a ton, about eight dollars a ton. It is as about six to eight.

Q. Is eight dollars a ton the ordinary price of the coal they use?

A. I should say that would be a low price.

Q. What is the usual price of the coal that has been used to your knowledge in those places?

A. I don't know. I have never seen or noticed any of their coal bills. I simply made inquiry in reference to the comparative cost of the coal they use.

Q. Have you ever examined to see what the comparative cost was of the coal which you use and the coal which the Boston Gas Light Co. use?

A. I have never noticed any of the Boston Gas Light Co.'s coal. I know nothing about it, and therefore cannot compare it.

Q. Have you ever examined to satisfy yourself what was the cost to the Boston Gas Light Co. of the gas which they manufacture?

A. I never have, sir. I am not a stockholder, and I have never had an opportunity to know what their gas costs them in any way; have never made particular inquiries in regard to the cost of gas to the Boston Gas Light Co. per cubic foot, or per thousand cubic feet. I have made general inquiries in reference to what was about the scale of cost.

Q. Have you any other information, Mr. Baldwin, on which to base your judgment, that gas can be profitably made by the new company, beyond your experience in connection with these public institutions?

A. I don't profess to be an expert as to the manufacture of gas. I have never had any experience of any kind; but I have taken hold of many business projects with, perhaps, as little practical knowledge as I have of the manufacture of gas, which have proved successful. On general principles, sir, I believe that in the case of a company that has gone on fifty-four years without competition, and become so large a monopoly as the Boston Gas-Light Company is, an honorable competition would do it no injury; and certainly the Citizens' Company, if they manage their business as judiciously as the Boston Gas-Light Company do, would prove a successful enterprise, and a benefit to the citizens.

Q. I take it you propose to put your money into this company for the purpose of permanently supplying the citizens of Boston with cheaper gas, and thus making money,— isn't that your object?

A. To state to you precisely my feelings in regard to investing money in this project, which I propose to do (of course the Board of Aldermen will see that proper provisions are made), I feel that, in making the investment, I want a fair return for my money at the same time.

Q. Let me interrupt you one moment. What do you call a "fair return" for your money?

A. A fair return for all my investment.

Q. Well, what?

A. I think a fair return will be all that the business can yield by judicious management, and by courtesy extended towards the citizens, our customers; but I should not, of course, be confined to any particular per cent. I think it would be the policy of the company to offer the product to the citizens at as low or a lower price than they have been in the habit of having it; and it would be the policy of the company to place the pipes where the takers would be numerous, and the policy of the company to make themselves popular.

Q. Would three per cent on your money satisfy you?

A. If you will step into my office to-morrow, I will give you my rates. I don't believe that I am called upon to answer that question, although if the Board require it of me I certainly shall be very happy to.

THE CHAIRMAN. The Chair will state that Mr. Baldwin is here to answer such questions as the counsel or members of the Board may propose to him, unless objection is made by his counsel. It is supposed that if any improper question is asked, they will object.

MR. COLLINS. I don't think that is a proper question.

MR. MORSE. So long as this objection is taken, I desire very respectfully to say to the Board, that we do not wish to take up their time for a moment with any question that shall not seem to them to be proper; but we do desire to probe this matter to the bottom, and ascertain what is the basis, what is the foundation of this movement. We do not suppose that this is an application on the part of certain gentlemen to supply gas at a lower rate than the Gas Company now supply it to the city, unless they can make a profit from it, and we think it is a perfectly proper question to ask this gentleman and others who are proposing to put in their money, what rate of interest they propose to get out of this; what will satisfy them as a reasonable rate. If the Board say that it is not proper to go into that question, of course I shall follow their direction.

Mr. Baldwin. I should be entirely willing, if it is the decision of the Board that that is a proper question to be answered, to respond what in my judgment is a fair return for an investment in a corporation.

Q. My question is not so general as that. My question is this: The witness has stated that he is a subscriber to this corporation, and proposes to put in all the money he can get; and I don't know but he said, all the money he can borrow. Now, I want to know whether this money is to be put in for the benefit of the city, or as a business investment; and if as a business investment, what rate of interest he expects to realize from it; and then the Aldermen may have some means of forming an opinion as to whether the city will save any money by granting this privilege which is asked for.

Mr. Collins. As counsel for the Citizens' Gas Light Company, I will say that the Boston Gas Light Company need not be solicitous about the corporators making any money. They propose to invest their money, and take the risk of a fair return. What they will be satisfied with, it strikes me, is an impertinent question; and therefore I object to the witness answering it.

Alderman Peters. I should like to ask if the objection is to the question whether three per cent would satisfy him, or what per cent will satisfy him. It seems to me that the question what per cent will be satisfactory, is a fair question.

It is not like asking what a man would be willing to lend money for; but it is asking what he thinks would be a fair return. He might say that a part of the return would be the satisfaction in getting gas cheaper, and in seeing the city supplied more cheaply. It seems to me a fair question would be what he would consider a fair per centage of dividend on the stock.

A. My own impression is, that a return on an investment of that description, of from eight to ten per cent. would be a fair return. That is, I think that if I invested in this company, I should be entirely satisfied with that percentage.

Q. (By MR. MORSE.) Ten per cent?

A. From eight to ten.

Q. You wouldn't take, as you stated a moment ago, all the money you had, and all you could get, and put it into an enterprise of this kind, unless you felt you could realize that return?

A. I mean to say, that I know of my own knowledge that this project is started in good faith on the part of the corporators, to provide the citizens of Boston with gas at as low a price as possible, with a fair return on the money invested. I know it is started in good faith, and as one of these corporators, having some pride as to the character of my associates, and especially of their character as associates, my last dollar should go to make the enterprise a respectable one.

Q. May I ask you how much you have subscribed to the present $5,000?

MR. HYDE. I don't think that question has any thing to do with the good faith of these people. Of course, you understand perfectly well that that amount is merely enough to organize for the purpose of having a corporate existence. These parties say they are ready to furnish a million dollars. If they do not furnish it, do not build their works, then of course, nobody is harmed, no streets are dug up, and no injury is done; but the question, what proportion of $5,000 he has put in, is not a pertinent question. That is a merely formal amount; I mean it is no substantial part of the capital of this company. Mr. Baldwin has told you, and it is perfectly well understood, that he is ready to put his money in here.

Mr. Morse. Are you willing to produce the subscription list to the amount of a million dollars.

Mr. Hyde. I say this, that if any gentleman of this Board of Aldermen wishes to see this subscription list, he can have the opportunity. This company comes here in good faith. They are here proposing to build these works, to put in their money and take the risk, to lay their pipes, and undertake to furnish the city of Boston with gas at a lower price than they have it now, and of a better quality. They are ready to put a million dollars into it, they are ready to risk their money, and when the proper time comes, we shall show the list. If we do not raise that money the works will not be built, and they know it as well as we do. I stand here as counsel, not as one of the corporators. I am not personally interested in the matter, and I say that these corporators are ready to come forward in good faith and furnish an article which is as necessary to every person in this city, poor and rich, as the water of Cochituate lake. We come here in good faith. We have subscribed our money, and I want to know if any thing more can be asked of any one. It is not your money, nor any one else's money that we propose to put in ; it is our own money. If they question our good faith, and want to know where this money is to come from, if they want a hundred thousand dollars deposited with the City Treasurer as a guarantee of our good faith, they can have it to-morrow. We are not here to get a franchise for the purpose of peddling it around the town, or any thing of that kind. We come here as substantial citizens, to invest our money. As well might the Legislature ask who are going to own the stock of the Boston & Albany R. R. when it goes for a charter, as these gentlemen ask the names of the subscribers to the Citizens' Gas Light Co. But, as I say, if the Board of Aldermen wants a list of the people who propose to subscribe to this stock, they can have it, but I do not think it is right for the rival corporation to come in and ask the question. It is not a pertinent question.

Mr. MORSE. I have not sought to discuss any question which will hereafter arise; but it seems to me that it is perfectly proper to ask these petitioners, who come here asking this Board for a power which has never been delegated by any city government anywhere, to any corporation, to satisfy the Board of their ability to carry out the work which they seek permission of this Board to do. The spectacle is simply ridiculous of this company, that has paid in $5,000, applying to the city government for leave to dig up every street and every alley-way in the city of Boston, including not merely the main part of the city, but all the suburbs; and when it is said that the $5,000 is only a nominal sum which they fixed so as to escape paying taxes to the State, then, I say, show precisely what you have; and we are met with the objection that it is a piece of impertinence to inquire into their private affairs. All that I desire to do is to get from these gentlemen a statement of just what their condition is. I ask them to produce their subscription-paper, and let us see who are the persons who have subscribed, and what are the amounts subscribed, and all about it. And when my friend says that the Legislature are not in the habit of exacting such terms, I beg to correct him. I believe it is not an uncommon thing, in cases where a peculiar charter is asked for, for the Legislature, or a committee, to insist upon being thoroughly satisfied of the good faith of those who ask for it, and of their ability to carry on the work which they seek to get incorporated to do. Now, in this particular case, my friend does not pretend that a company, with a capital of $5,000, could carry on this business. I say, therefore, that it is reasonable that he or his clients should produce the real subscription-paper on which they rely.

Mr. HYDE. I understand that the Legislature, when it desires to make sure, does this: it puts a condition into the bill that the company shall not organize and go forward until a certain amount of capital is actually paid in. Now, we are perfectly willing that this Board should put in the privilege they grant us this condition, that we shall have no right to touch a street in Boston until a million dollars of actual cash is paid in. You may put that condition in, and we are entirely content that a million dollars shall first be paid in in actual money before any right to touch a street shall attach. If we do not pay it in, we shall never get any right.

MR. MORSE. Do you say that you have paid in subscriptions to the amount of a million dollars?

MR. HYDE. I say this, that if anybody questions our good faith, or if the Board of Aldermen think it is for the interest of the city that a guarantee should be put into the privilege they grant us in that form, they can put it in.

MR. MORSE. I would like to ask my brother Hyde, if he has ever seen such a paper?

MR. HYDE. I have not. I have never asked the question if I could see the paper. I asked these gentlemen, when I met them, if they were in a position to go forward and carry out what they proposed; and they assured me they were, and named the several sums which they had obtained subscriptions for. I took their word for it; and when Mr. Baldwin made that statement to me, I was content.

Q. (By MR. MORSE.) Have you had any experienced man in the manufacture of gas make any estimates for the benefit of your associates and yourself, as to the cost of making gas to supply the city?

A. I will say, in reply to that question, that we have occasionally met as corporators, and reported to each other, and discussed from time to time the probable result of making gas, commencing with a capital such as we have a right to start with under the general law of the State; but of course we haven't brought the thing down to a nicety, for much depends upon what our works cost, and there are so many —

Q. Well, have you estimated, for instance, how much your works will cost?

A. Not to a cent; we couldn't estimate it.

Q. Well, have you estimated it within $50,000?

A. I don't think we have. I don't think it would be possible for us to estimate it.

Q. Have you made any estimate of how much it would cost to lay the pipes, or how much the pipes themselves would cost?

A. That matter hasn't been discussed to any extent.

Q. Have you had any figures from any source which have been laid before you and your associates, to show the probable cost of the manufacture of gas to the company?

A. We haven't had any figures laid before us which show the exact cost.

Q. Have you had any which show the approximate cost?

A. We have had statements made as to the approximate cost.

Q. From whom?

A. Not from one party, but from many parties.

Q. From whom, for one?

A. Well, so far as the cost of manufacturing gas is concerned, for my own part, I have talked with our people down at Deer Island, and our people at the House of Correction.

Q. That is very indefinite. Whom do you mean by "our people"?

A. Well, I have talked with one member of this Board, who is on the Board of Directors, Alderman Powers. I have talked with other gentlemen upon the Board, and I must confess I was somewhat astonished, to know how cheaply gas could be manufactured of the quality which is manufactured there; and this led me to make other inquiries; and I have also talked with two or three New-York gentlemen, Mr. Kennedy, and two or three gentlemen from New York, whose names I forget.

Q. (By Mr. Putnam.) Do I understand you to have had any estimates made of what it would cost you to furnish gas?

A. We haven't had any estimates made to bring the cost down to the lowest possible figure, or to a particular figure.

Q. Well, have you had any estimates made at what rate you could furnish gas to the citizens of Boston?

A. Well, we have estimated that we could furnish gas to

the citizens of Boston at a profit, and furnish it at less than the Boston Gas Light Company at present furnish it to the citizens of Boston.

Q. You have had such an estimate as that made, have you?

A. Yes, sir.

Q. Who made it?

A. Well, if I have replied incorrectly, I will explain myself. There have been no figures made, that is, it has not been reduced down to a point, because that is impossible, until we know what our works cost us, and until we know what it will cost to lay our pipes, because these expenses enter into the cost.

Q. Then you haven't had any calculation made of what your works would cost you?

A. No, sir.

Q. Or of what it would cost you per foot or per mile to lay your main pipes?

A. No, sir.

Q. Nor of what the pipes themselves would cost you, have you?

A. We have not; that is, not what they would cost per mile.

Q. These are the principal elements, are they not, in determining what you are going to be able to afford your gas at?

A. They are to a certain degree, but we haven't considered them. I answer your questions as well as I can, but I have not posted myself on these points. There are gentlemen here who can answer such questions, and we should be glad to have you inquire of them.

Q. Then these estimates have been made, but you can't give them?

A. I say that these estimates have been made, or they can be made, but I am not sufficiently acquainted with the points to give you satisfactory evidence. We have other evidence here, which will be introduced, which will be more satisfactory to you than mine.

Q. You don't propose to cover the whole city, suburbs, new parts, and all, with pipes immediately, do you?
A. I don't suppose we should.
Q. Have you formed any plan as to where you will begin to lay your pipes — what district you will first occupy?
A. Where our business interests would lead us.
Q. Of course, that goes without saying; but have you made up your minds what part of the city, — that is, where your best interests would first lead you?
A. I can't answer. We have never made up our minds, from the fact that we are looking out for sites. We have several in mind.
Q. I don't mean sites for your works; but have you made up your minds in what part of the city you will commence?
A. We have made up our minds to commence within the city of Boston.
Q. Within the old city?
A. Not within the old city.
Q. Within the present city?
A. Within the present city.
Q. You haven't made up your minds as to any particular territory within the present city limits which you intend to occupy first?
A. There has been no action upon that point.
Q. And no decision in your own mind?
A. No decision in my own mind.
Q. Are you willing to state what your individual subscription to this million dollars is?
A. I am willing to state precisely what I stated to the committee of the Legislature last winter, if it is deemed to be a pertinent question.
Q. If you are not willing to state it, Mr. Baldwin, I won't put it. I ask you if you are willing to state what is your own individual subscription to this million dollars that has been spoken of?
A. THE CHAIRMAN. The Chair would state that in his opinion it is a question entirely optional with the witness to

answer or not. It is not pertinent to this investigation; but unless some member of the Board objects, the Chair will allow the inquiries to take a very wide range. If any gentleman objects, then it will be time for the Chair to rule.

MR. BALDWIN. If the Chairman decides that it is a pertinent question, I am ready and willing to make the answer; but if it isn't a pertinent question, I don't care to advertise the amount that I propose to subscribe.

Q. The question I asked was, how much you have subscribed to this million dollars, if you are willing to answer. If not, I will waive the question.

A. I shall decline to answer, except the Chair rules that it is a pertinent question.

Q. I don't ask the Chair to rule. If you don't wish to answer it, I will waive it.

A. I don't wish to answer it.

Q. But whatever sum you have subscribed, you propose to put in, and are willing to put in on such vague information as you have already stated, as to the cost of the works, and the profit that can be made?

A. I am.

Q. Have you considered what the effect is likely to be, of laying pipes alongside of the Boston Gas Light Company's pipes through the city, as to the number of takers that you would be likely to get? Suppose you laid your pipes alongside of the pipes of the Boston Gas Light Company, through the streets of the city, do you suppose you would be able to get the greater part of their customers away from them?

A. That is a question I will answer in this way, sir. I came to Boston a poor boy; and when I started a store, there were a good many large ones right by the side of me. It didn't prevent my starting a store though; and I have been moderately successful, though there are very many men who have been more successful.

Q. Do you think that is a parallel case?

A. I think it is a similar case.

Q. There are probably four million dollars invested in

gas works within the limits of the city of Boston. Do you think that if there were four million dollars more invested right alongside of the existing pipes, through the same territory, it would be profitable for all the capital invested, and that the citizens would get their gas cheaper?

A. I haven't a question about it.

ALDERMAN BROOKS. The counsel inquired very minutely as regards the quality of coal which you propose to use. Now what kind of coal have you used at the public institutions?

A. I don't know anything concerning the quality of coal; but if I understand the true economy in the manufacture of gas, it is to use the best coal that can be purchased, rather than to buy coal of inferior quality; but not being an expert upon matters of that kind, as to what quality of coal will make the most or the least, I will not undertake to answer; for I know that we have evidence which will be much more intelligible to the Board than any I can give them in that respect.

ALDERMAN PETERS. In this estimate of the cost of gas manufactured at Deer Island, you don't count in the labor, and you don't allow any interest on the works at all?

A. I have so stated. There is no calculation made of the interest on the cost of the works, and no calculation of the cost of labor outside of the skilled labor; but the matter could be brought down, I think, to the inside, from the fact that every day's work is placed upon the reports; so that the Board could at any time get at the exact cost in that way.

Q. (By MR. COLLINS.) The question has been asked, where you propose to lay pipes, and whom you propose to supply first. Is it the intention of your corporation to go wherever the Board will give them authority to go, — to South Boston, East Boston, and other parts of the city, — everywhere where they can find customers, and get authority to go?

A. Yes, sir; it is.

Q. You propose to take your own risk in reference to getting customers in the city of Boston?

5

A. We propose to take our own risk in reference to getting customers in the city of Boston. We propose to take our own risk with reference to getting the city itself as a customer.

Q. You propose to come over and relieve us a little in South Boston from the company that Mr. Putnam represents?

A. Yes, sir; we do.

TESTIMONY OF LEOPOLD MORSE.

Q. (By Mr. Hyde.) You are one of the corporators?
A. I am.
Q. Are you acting in good faith?
A. I am.
Q. Are you proposing to put your own money into this company?
A. I am.
Q. Are you proposing to go forward in good faith, and furnish the citizens of Boston with gas, and supply them in a manner that shall be satisfactory to them?
A. I so understand.

Cross-Examination.

Q. (By Mr. Morse.) Do you feel as delicate as the other gentlemen about stating how much you have subscribed?
A. I do not.
Q. Then won't you state how much you have subscribed?
A. I have subscribed in the same manner that subscriptions of that kind are generally made ; the same as I subscribed ($50,000) to a bank, with no idea of taking it, didn't intend to take it, didn't expect to take it, but I held myself responsible for it, knowing or believing that my friends and

associates would take up the balance when the proper time came; and when they got the charter, I took my $10,000, and my friends were very glad to take the $40,000. The subscription I have made to this company would be on the same principle exactly.

Q. How much have you subscribed?

A. I haven't subscribed any more than what I subscribed on the original subscription.

Q. You haven't seen the paper containing subscriptions to the amount of a million dollars, then?

A. I have not, but it is generally understood; I haven't seen a man on the street who has known my name was on the petition that you have seen to-day, but what is ready to subscribe any amount I require.

Q. Is there any such paper in existence?

A. I don't know.

Q. Do you believe there is?

A. I don't know any thing about it.

Q. You have heard the statement that there is a paper subscribing a million dollars?

A. I have.

Q. Do you believe there is?

A. I don't know any thing about it. It isn't very likely I should stand here and say my associates lie.

Q. You haven't seen it?

A. I never saw it.

Q. You haven't seen any subscription, have you?

A. I have seen the original one.

Q. How much was that?

A. Five hundred dollars I have agreed to pay.

Q. Have you seen any paper with Mr. Carpenter's name on it to the extent of $250,000.

A. I just told you I hadn't seen that paper.

Q. You are one of the corporators of this company?

A. I am.

Q. Have you gone into the question as to the expense of manufacturing gas?

A. I have not. I generally form my opinion on general impressions of the public at large and my own judgment, and I am satisfied that if we could get the right to do what we propose to do, that I could make a good deal of money out of my investment.

Q. How much?

A. I don't know. I can't tell how successful we might be. Our pipes might all burst the first night, and the citizens might not look so favorably upon us as we expect, and might not take the gas from us, but, on general impressions, I am satisfied we can make a success of it.

Q. You don't go into it so much for the public good as some of our associates?

A. I am not so much of a philanthropist as your corporation is, but the public might get as much benefit through us as they do through you.

Q. Have you had any estimate prepared for you by anybody, of the cost of manufacturing gas?

A. No more than I would if a person came into my place of business and asked me the price of a suit of clothes. I might go to my foreman; for I am not a tailor myself, although I am engaged in the business; and, on the same principle, I have seen parties from New York who gave me the general idea that the cost of producing gas depended upon the price of coal, which may cost eight dollars a ton this year and eighteen dollars next. The cost varies more or less with the price of coal and the price of labor; but I don't think the price of labor now has any thing to do with what it will cost, because we don't expect to get our works done to-day, nor to-morrow, nor next year.

Q. Do you propose to do any thing until you have been to the Legislature for an increase of capital?

A. I shall do whatever the parties think best to do. I believe in the enterprise.

Q. You have formed no opinion yourself of the cost of these different things?

A. I have formed the general opinion that people have,

that the thing is very profitable, otherwise you wouldn't be here opposing it.

Q. And so you think that you can make some profit in competition?

A. Well, we can try.

Q. And you propose to have the city of Boston give you leave to dig up the streets in order that you may have an opportunity to try it?

A. I have the same rights that you have; and I propose, as a large tax-payer, to come in here and demand my rights.

Q. And one of those rights you consider to be the right to dig up the streets of the city?

A. As far as it may be proper under their direction to do it.

Q. Then what you ask is to try an experiment?

A. If we fail that is our loss, and not the city's loss.

Q. Who is to pay the loss incurred by digging up the streets?

A. If the city require us to do so we will pay it.

Q. But the citizens are incommoded. Who is to pay them on that account?

A. The citizens are incommoded by you in the same way.

TESTIMONY OF JOHN P. KENNEDY.

Q. (By Mr. Collins.) You are a resident where?

A. New York.

Q. And your business?

A. I am a gas engineer.

Q. Will you state how long you have been a gas engineer?

A. About twenty-five years.

Q. Will you state where you have constructed gas works and laid pipes in different cities of the Union?

A. That would be rather a tedious job, I have built so many. I have built them through the United States, including California.

Q. Have you built in San Francisco?
A. I have, sir.
Q. Any other city in California?
A. No, sir.
Q. When did you build in San Francisco?
A. In 1854 and '55.
Q. Coming toward the east, where did you build?
A. The next I built was in New Jersey.
Q. What city?
A. Newark, sir.
Q. How large is the city of Newark?
A. About one hundred and twenty thousand population.
Q. Have you built in New York?
A. I have.
Q. What works have you built in New York?
A. I built the Metropolitan and the Mutual.
Q. When did you build the Metropolitan?
A. That was during the war, 1862 and '63.
Q. How many companies did the Metropolitan make in New-York City when it was built?
A. It was the fourth company.
Q. Have you built gas works in New York since?
A. Yes, sir, I have built the Mutual Works.
Q. Are the Mutual Works large works?
A. They are of the capacity of between three and four millions per day.
Q. Are the Metropolitan Works large?
A. Yes, sir, they are very near the same size, I should udge.
Q. Are either of those gas works as large as the Boston Gas Works?
A. That I can't say, sir, I am not conversant with the Boston Gas Works.
Q. Do you hold any position in either of those companies?

A. Well, I am managing director of the Mutual Gas Light Company.

Q. What is the capital of the Mutual Company?

A. Five millions.

Q. Have you built any works in Philadelphia?

A. No, sir.

Q. In Detroit?

A. Yes, sir. I built the works for a company in Detroit.

Q. When was that?

A. That was about two years ago. They were finished about two years ago.

Q. Is that the only company in Detroit?

A. No, sir, there are two there. This is a competing company.

Q. Does this company lay their pipes in the same streets with the other company?

A. Yes, sir.

Q. The old company and the new company have their pipes laid down side by side in Detroit?

A. Yes, sir.

Q. Supply people and stores in the same streets?

A. Yes, sir.

Q. Any great difficulty about that?

A. No, sir.

Q. Perfectly practicable?

A. Entirely so, sir.

Q. In New York, you say, there are four companies?

A. There are five companies now.

Q. Are the pipes of any of those companies laid down in the same streets?

A. Yes, sir; the Mutual Company's pipes extend through three of the districts. That is, New York is districted into four districts, and each of the old companies is circumscribed by certain boundaries; but the Mutual Company, being a competing company, their pipes pass through three of those districts.

Q. Then the Board are to understand that there were four companies in New York before the Mutual was started and the city was divided into four districts, and the Mutual Company has equal rights with the other companies in three of the districts?

A. In all four of the districts, but they occupy only three.

Q. Do you find any difficulty in laying pipes and supplying customers?

A. Not the slightest.

Q. Has the Mutual Company been a success?

A. We think so.

Q. Whom do you supply there?

A. Well, we supply almost all the hotels, theatres, billiard saloons, lager-beer gardens, a large portion of the stores, and a great many private dwellings.

Q. How many million feet did you sell last year?

A. We sold nearly 400,000,000.

Q. So that in New York and in Detroit, at all events, there are companies having their pipes in the same streets, competing for the same customers, and there is no difficulty experienced?

A. No, sir.

Q. Do you know any other case of the kind?

A. I do not, sir.

Q. You have been familiar with the manufacture of gas for how long?

A. For nearly twenty-five years.

Q. Have you advised this corporation?

A. Well, sir, I have had some conversation with them; nothing very special.

Q. Your business is that of gas engineer; you construct gas works, and they have consulted you?

A. That was my business; yes, sir.

Q. And you can answer all questions about the price of gas, the cost of the construction of works, and the cost of manufacturing gas?

A. I can answer all proper questions.

MR. COLLINS. — Now, Mr. Morse, if you want to know any thing about gas works, the manufacture of gas, the cost of making it, or the profits, that you cannot get from your company, Mr. Kennedy will answer the questions.

CROSS-EXAMINATION.

Q. (BY MR. MORSE.) What is the price of gas in New York?

A. The price of gas is $2.75 per thousand.

Q. Is that the price of all the companies?

A. Yes, sir.

Q. What was the price before this Mutual Co. came in to compete?

A. Well, sir, the price was $3.00, but you are aware that they took off the government tax, and that made it $2.75.

Q. Was it $2.75 to the consumers?

A. When we started the price was $3.00, because the government tax was on.

Q. You charged $3.00 at that time?

A. We charged the same as the other companies.

Q. You took off the government tax, and consequently reduced the price to $2.75?

A. Yes, sir, the same as they did.

Q. Then the only reduction since the competing company started there has been the taking off of the government-tax?

A, The only nominal reduction was in the price of gas per thousand. There is a reduction beyond that.

Q. What is that?

A. The quality of the gas, sir.

Q. A reduction in the quality of the gas?

A. No, sir, an improvement in the quality, whereby the bills are reduced beyond the reduction in the price per thousand.

Q. In both companies?

A. No, sir. I said that there was another reduction to be made in the price of gas, beyond the nominal price per thousand.

Q. You don't say that there has been an actual reduction in the price, but simply that there has been an improvement in the quality of the gas?

A. Well, I can say more than that. I say there has been a reduction in the price, and a further reduction in the price by reason of the better gas made by the Mutual Co. That is, the bills are smaller.

Q. Do you consider your gas better than that made by the Manhattan Co.?

A. I do, sir, most decidedly.

Q. How much do the Manhattan Company sell a year?

A. It is a difficult figure to carry exactly in your head; but, approximately, I suppose, they sell about 1,200,000,000 feet.

Q. And how much do you sell?

A. We sell about 400,000,000. I think we shall reach 450,000,000 this year, probably 500,000,000.

Q. The Manhattan Company is one of the companies with which you compete?

A. Yes, sir.

Q. And they sell 1,200,000,000; about three times as much as you do.

A. Yes, sir.

Q. And yet you say you think your gas is cheaper than theirs?

A. Yes, sir, I do.

Q. Has your company paid a dividend?

A. No, sir, they have not.

Q. When did they start in their business?

A. Well, sir, they have been in operation over two years.

Q. They have been in operation over two years and haven't paid a dividend yet?

A. No, sir. I can give you a reason for that. The

reason is this: that, when we built our works, business pressed itself so rapidly upon us that we were obliged to increase the capacity of our works. We had absorbed our capital, and were obliged to use our earnings to increase the works; consequently, we made the stockholders no dividends, because we had to spend it on the works.

Q. How much have you spent for works?
A. I can't say that.
Q. In round numbers?
A. I suppose we have spent about $3,000,000.
Q. And your capital is $5,000,000?
A. Yes, sir.
Q. How much has been paid in in cash?
A. There was fifty per cent paid in, — $2,500,000.
Q. Then do I understand you that you have spent for your works half a million more than has been paid in in cash?
A. I think we have, sir, as nearly as I can remember.
Q. Well, was stock issued for $ 5,000,000?
A. Stock was issued for $5,000,000.
Q. On payment of fifty per cent.
A. Yes, sir.
Q. Is the cost of coal higher in New York than in Boston, or lower?
A. That I am not prepared to say, never having purchased any coal here.
Q. Do you understand why it is that the Boston Gas Company furnishes gas at $2.50, when you are furnishing it at $2.75?
A. On general terms, I think you get your coal cheaper than we do in New York. I think you use a great deal of the Provinces' coal.
Q. What do you pay for coal there, say the Provincial coal?
A. Well, I never bought any of that, sir. I never admired it for making gas.
Q. What do you use?

A. Pennsylvania coal.
Q. What kinds of Pennsylvania coal?
A. We use the Westmoreland, the Penn, and the Yonghiogheny.
Q. What do you pay for the Westmoreland?
A. $7.50 this year.
Q. And for the Penn?
A. They are all the same price.
Q. Have you any doubt that those coals would cost more here than in New York?
A. Well, I don't know, sir; that would depend upon the shippers. That I am not prepared to say. When the coal is put on board vessels, you know, it has the same handling whether you take it a little further or nearer.
Q. What part of the city are the pipes of the Mutual Company laid in?
A. Well, sir, the pipes extend from 65th Street, 3d Avenue, to Wall Street.
Q. The entire width of the city?
A. No, sir. We take the central part of the city.
Q. How many of the streets?
A. I can't pretend to tell you that.
Q. How many miles of pipe have you?
A. I think we have over seventy, sir. I beg gentlemen to remember that these are figures that are approximate. I desire to give the facts, but I can't give them to a fraction. I give them to you as nearly as I can.
Q. Give us approximately the number of miles that the other companies have laid?
A. I can't, sir; I suppose they have three or four hundred miles.
Q. When did this competing company that you speak of in Detroit begin business?
A. Just about two years ago, sir.
Q. Are the pipes laid, and the company at work?
A. Oh yes, sir. The works were begun the spring previously, and finished during that year. I built those

works in about eight calendar months, and put them in operation.

Q. What is the price of gas there?

A. The old company is selling it at two dollars a thousand, and the new company at one dollar a thousand to large consumers, and a dollar and a half to the smaller class.

Q. Has that company paid any dividend?

A. No, sir, it has not.

Q. Do you know what the cost of coal is there?

A. Yes, sir.

Q. What is it?

A. The coal that they have laid in for this winter the president informed me, cost him four dollars per ton (net ton) in Detroit.

Q. (By Mr. Putnam.) Have you made any estimate for these gentlemen of what it would cost to build works in Boston?

A. I haven't made any estimate. I haven't been called upon?

Q. (By Mr. Morse.) Are you interested in any way in the Boston Company?

A. I am not, sir. I am simply here by invitation, and hope to build their works if they build them.

Q. I mean in this proposed Citizens' Company?

A. No, sir. I propose to build the works for them if they favor me with the contract.

Q. You have never looked into the cost of manufacturing gas in Boston?

A. No, sir. It hasn't been necessary. I am pretty well posted on that.

Q. Have you estimated the cost of the works here that you propose to build?

A. No sir, I haven't estimated that.

Q. (By Mr. Collins.) I want to ask you one question. You have said that the gas supplied to New-York people by your company was cheaper, because the bills are less at the end of the month. I want the Board to understand precisely what you mean by that. Is it on account of the richness of the gas?

A. Yes, sir.

Q. Now suppose, Mr. Kennedy, that one company supplies a gas of fourteen-candle power, and another company supplies a gas of eighteen-candle power, and they are burned equally, which will register the most feet of gas?

A. The low-candle power, of course.

Q. And why?

A. Being thinner gas, it will go through the meter faster than the heavier gas.

Q. The lighter gas, the lower the candle power, the more the meter will register?

A. The more rapidly it passes through the meter, of course.

Q. In what proportion?

A. Well, sir, it is almost in the ratio of the candle power.

Q. That is, an eighteen-candle gas will register about how much in comparison with a fourteen-candle gas.

A. There will be about twenty-five per cent difference, I suppose, in the consumption.

Q. That is, you burn twenty-five per cent more of fourteen-candle power gas than of eighteen?

A. Yes, sir, to get the same light.

Q. And therefore the bills of the consumer, although he has better light, will be smaller at the end of the month?

A. Yes sir.

Q. That is, supposing this chandelier to burn gas of fourteen-candle. power and run a month, and then to run another month burning gas of eighteen-candle power, the bill for the eighteen-candle power gas, of greater brilliancy, will be only fourteen-eighteenths of the bill for the fourteen-candle power?

A. Yes, sir, approximately.

47

Q. Much has been said about the interruption to travel, and the great public nuisance of tearing up streets. I want to ask you whether in your experience in laying pipes for new companies in the different cities of this Union, you have heard any great complaint on that score, and whether it is probable, if new works are built in Boston, and pipes laid, there will be any serious interruption to business generally?

A. Of course some people would complain. There would be a little interruption, but it would only last about twenty-four hours. From the time of opening the streets to the time when the pavement was put down again would occupy about twenty-four hours. That would be all the inconvenience which the people would suffer. In New York, when we laid the pipes there, the people took it very good naturedly. They rather courted the inconveniences, because they thought they were going to have two companies, perhaps, in front of their houses, so that they could take their choice.

Q. Have you made any plans for the proposed works in Boston?

A. No, sir, I haven't.

Q. (By MR. MORSE.) What do you think of our streets in Boston as compared with the streets in New York?

A. Well, sir, I don't think they are as wide as our streets, or as straight.

Q. (By ALDERMAN POWER.) I understand you to say that you had some idea of the cost of gas works. Do you know how much the Boston Gas Light Company make?

A. No, sir. I saw a pamphlet here on Saturday of the consumption of gas here in Boston, in which it was stated that the consumption then was about six hundred and some millions feet; so that in general terms I should say that they sold about eight hundred million feet a year. I don't know the fact; it is mere guess work on my part, being a stranger here.

Q. Presuming that this company is managed well, what is your idea as to the cost of manufacturing the gas?

A. Well, sir, that is a matter I would rather not discuss, if you will excuse me. I am manager in a number of gas works, and I hold that the cost of their manufacture is their property, and not mine, and I have no right to dispense it without their authority; otherwise I would be most happy to state it. I wish to give you all the information I can, but I want to do it discreetly, and in a proper manner.

Q. You understand why I asked the question. There is some question as to whether or no there is a sufficient margin of profit to induce a competing company to go into this business?

A. Oh! yes, sir, I think there is. I think with works of modern construction, and managed with any sort of ability, that gas can be sold to satisfy the public, and have a margin of profit left.

Q. Well, sir, assuming that the new company can secure one half of the business of the city of Boston, what is your idea as to the company's constructing works to furnish that amount of gas?

A. Well, sir, it would take a good deal more money than this company have allotted to them in this privilege that they have; but I presume that if the authorities saw this company going to work in good earnest, and disposed to do what is right, they would help them out in the matter undoubtedly. That is my opinion about it. I only speak on general principles.

Q. You have no doubt, then, feeling that you know what the cost would be, that if the business was well conducted it would pay a good profit?

A. I have no doubt at all.

CROSS-EXAMINATION.

Q. (By MR. MORSE.) Have you formed an opinion as to the price at which the new company can sell gas?

A. No, sir, I have not. I want to answer every question that is proper, gentlemen, but I do not want to give the history of this business. I do not think it is proper; and, with all deference to you, I think it is a very improper question for you to ask me.

Q. You appear, Mr. Kennedy, in behalf of the gentlemen who desire to supply gas to the city?

A. No; I am here, at their request, to answer questions that may be put to me.

Q. I do not wish to put any improper questions to you; I simply want to know whether you are prepared to show at what price the new company can furnish gas to the city?

MR. COLLINS. I ought to object to that question. He is a constructor of gas-works, is employed in all the great cities to construct gas-works, and if he were to tell at what price gas could be manufactured and supplied, it might injure his business. I know Mr. Greenough has always refused to answer that question.

THE CHAIRMAN. It certainly is a proper question. It is just the information which this Board desire to have. We want to know whether gas could be furnished to the citizens of Boston at a profit at two dollars per thousand, instead of two dollars and fifty cents.

MR. KENNEDY. I will answer that if the gentlemen desire me to.

ALD. HALL. I would like to propound a question first, as it may lead to that in the end. I would like to know what the candle-power is of this gas which is now burning in this room?

A. I think it is good sixteen or seventeen candle gas.

Q. Will you state what candle-power your own gas is; I mean the gas of the Mutual Gas Light Company of New York.

A. Twenty-candle power.

Q. What is the gas of the other companies in opposition to yours?

A. From fourteen to sixteen and a half.

Q. Something similar to this?

A. Yes, sir.

Q. (By ALD. STEBBINS.) What is the cost of producing the gas furnished by the Mutual Company of New York?

A. I stated a short time ago that that information was not my property.

Q. I should like to have you state it to the Board.

A. I respectfully decline to do that.

Q. (By ALDERMAN PETERS.) What does the city of New York, in its corporate capacity, pay for the gas with which they light the streets?

A. That, sir, I can answer you very particularly, because I have been through several computations for the lighting of the streets of New York; that being my duty as the managing-director of the New York Mutual Gas Light Company. When we commenced our works in New York, the price of the gas burned in the street-lamps was $53 per lamp; that included the cost of lighting, extinguishing, and cleaning. The repairs on the lamps were performed by the companies; but the city authorities paid for them. When we came in competition for lighting the streets, the price was reduced to $33 per lamp, and they are now being lighted at that price in three of the districts. In the fourth, which is the extreme up-town and Harlem District, they get $39 a lamp, because there is no competition there; the Mutual pipes are not running in that district.

Q. Do you have any way of measuring the amount of gas that the lamps consume?

A. We do not in New York. We make a round bargain per lamp.

Q. As near as you can tell, what do you suppose $33 per lamp, making an allowance for lighting and cleaning, gives you per foot?

A. Well, sir, the burners consume three feet per hour. It is very easily figured. We light during the entire year, moonlight or not. We light up moonlight nights as well as dark nights. At $32 per lamp, we get $2.75 per thousand cubic feet for our gas. I would state further, that we have 18,000 street-lamps in New York, in the parks and in the streets; and $20 per lamp less is considerable saving to the city of New York.

Q. (By ALDERMAN CUTTER.) I understood you to answer Alderman Power that you thought that gas could be furnished at less than $2.50 per thousand, with a profit. I would like to ask you if, in answering that question, you included a dividend to the stockholders, and, if any, how much?

A. Now that would be just as difficult for me to answer, almost, as to stand on my head, because the cost of the works enters into this calculation and the customers that a competing company will obtain. Those two points would have to be determined, and, until they were determined, it would be impossible for me to answer.

Q. You answered that you thought gas could be produced at a less price. On what do you base that judgment? Where do you get that from?

A. Well, I get it in this way. I was asked the question, and I inferred I was placed in the position of the Boston Gas Light Company. I was going to answer, when some gentleman interrupted, that I would very much like to take the lighting of the city of Boston for a good deal less than $2.50 per thousand; but how much, I cannot say. Standing here and making statements, I must be very careful what I say. I want to state facts, and I want to give you all the information that I can; but I want to do it properly, and without prejudice to my friends with whom I am associated in the north and west.

Q. You have said that the companies you have been interested in have paid no dividends. Now, what I want to know is, if you can furnish gas cheaper than $2.50 per thousand and pay a dividend?

A. I said that the reason the New York Mutual Company did not pay any dividend was because they had to take their earnings to enlarge their works, and, consequently, a dividend had to be postponed until it could be earned again.

Q. (By ALD. BROOKS.) In your judgment, could gas be manufactured by this new corporation, and furnished to the citizens of Boston and to the city with a profit, at $2.00 per thousand, instead of $2.50?

A. Yes, sir, I think so.

Q. (By MR. MORSE.) And pay what dividend?

A. I can only repeat what I said, sir : I cannot state that.

Q. Do you think it would pay any dividend?

A. Yes, sir.

Q. About how much?

A. Well, now, I don't know your name, sir ; but I infer that you are well posted on gas ; and you do not want any information from me. You do not require any ; you know all about that.

Q. That is not quite a fair answer, Mr. Kennedy, that you have made.

A. Well, if you will tell me what your works earn at $2.50 per thousand, I will answer the question; but I cannot answer it now.

Q. My question is this : You said, in answer to Alderman Brooks, that you thought gas could be furnished by the new company with a profit at $2.00 per thousand?

A. Yes, sir.

Q. Now I ask you, how much dividend you think the company could pay its stockholders, and furnish gas at $2.00 per thousand?

A. Well, it would be simply a matter of opinion; there would be no matter of fact about it. It would be assertion on my part.

Q. Well, what is your opinion?

A. Well, I think they could get at least simple interest on their money.

Q. Six per cent?

A. Seven per cent; that is what we call simple interest where I live.

Q. You said a moment ago that you estimated the illuminating power of the gas in this room at sixteen or seventeen candles?

A. Yes, sir.

Q. I suppose you made this statement simply from general observation?

A. Yes, sir; I can tell pretty near.

Q. (By ALDERMAN HALL.) I would like to ask what the illuminating power is?

MR. GREENOUGH. [After consulting the superintendent.] It is eighteen and a half.

Q. (By ALDERMAN PETERS.) Has your company any funded or floating debt?

A. Yes, sir; we have bonds.

Q. That represents the money put into the works?

A. Yes, sir.

Q. (By ALDERMAN STEBBINS.) How much, in the way of profits, have you added to your construction account?

A. I should be telling my private business affairs if I told you that.

Q. We want to get at, in some way, what the cost of gas will be?

A. Gentlemen, I don't think you can get that out of me.

ALDERMAN WORTHINGTON. I think we are talking about a great deal, without coming to the point. These gentlemen come to the city of Boston, and ask us to permit them to take up the streets and put in new gas-pipes, and promise us that they will furnish gas at a less price than the present company; and claim that they can do that and pay a profit to their stockholders. Now, that is the direct point that we want here. If I vote to give this company leave to take up our streets, I must be sure that they can furnish gas at a less price, and furnish it at a profit, so that we shall have ever hereafter an independent company — a company that pays dividends; so that the stock will not be sold out to the Boston Gas Light Company, and so that we shall not have, in a few years, only one gas company; and that, too, after the citizens have submitted to the taking up of their streets; for if they once submit to the digging up their streets, and afterwards the two companies are consolidated, we shall never have another opposition company started. Now I desire that this company may present their case exactly to this point. I think it is the point we want to know here — what they can furnish gas for to the citizens of Boston, and pay a profit — how much less than the old company now charge? Let the witness answer the questions which bear upon these points. That is the information we want to get here to-night. I do not want all this conversation about "I don't like to answer that question, this question, or the other." I must be convinced of that one thing before I vote to give another gas company the right to take up our streets and put down their pipes: that they can furnish gas at a less price than the old company; or, if it is the fact that that cannot be done, I want the old company to come here and prove it. I want all the facts before I vote; no equivocation, no hesitation; but the solid facts, and nothing less.

Mr. Collins. Mr. Kennedy, the question is this — whether you can guarantee that this new company can furnish gas, if they get this right, to the consumers, at a less price per thousand than the old company, and of better quality? Will you answer that question?

A. Yes, sir; I say they can.

Q. (By Mr. Putnam). Do you mean that answer to apply to the whole city, including the outlying wards, or only the city proper?

A. Of course I do not expect that the new company would get all the business of Boston; but presuming that they would get a fair share of the business, it is based upon that, sir.

Q. My question is this: It has been testified, I believe, that the Boston Gas Light Co. furnish gas at $2.50 per thousand; you say that the new company could furnish it cheaper. Do you mean to testify that the new gas company can furnish gas to the citizens of the whole city, including the outlying wards, Brighton, West Roxbury, Dorchester, East Boston, South Boston, and Charlestown, at a lower price than $2.50 per thousand?

A. Yes, sir; I do.

Q. You understand what the extent of the city is now?

A. Well, I do, in general terms. I do not, of course, being a stranger, understand it perfectly. I have ridden round the city; but of course I am not as well conversant with it as other persons are.

Q. Do you mean to testify that the new company can furnish gas to the citizens at a less price than $2.50 per thousand, outside the densely populated parts of the city?

Mr. COLLINS. The Boston Gas Light Co. does not furnish it there.

Mr. PUTNAM. But your company seeks leave to go everywhere within the city limits, including Brighton, West Roxbury, and everywhere else.

Q. Do you think gas can be furnished in the country at a lower price than that?

A. Well, sir, if I was conversant with the place, I could answer better.

TESTIMONY OF W. W. GREENOUGH.

Q. (By Mr. HYDE.) Will you state what is the present price of the gas furnished by the Boston Gas Light Co.?

A. $2.50 per thousand to the private consumer.

Q. Will you state what that costs the company?

A. I cannot state it.

Q. Will you state as nearly as you can?

A. Well, as nearly as possible, the difference between the cost of the gas and the price at which it was furnished during the last six months of 1873 and the first six months of 1874, was not enough to pay 10 per cent dividend to the stockholders. I do not know what it costs: that comes as near to it as I can give you now.

Q. Do you keep any record in your works of the cost of the gas from day to day?

A. No, that is impossible.

Q. Well, nor in any length of time?

A. The constant items of cost are made up without allowing interest on the capital every six months.

Q. By reference to your books, can you tell for any six months what the cost of your gas was without the capital?

A. Yes, sir.

Q. You have the items that go into that cost?

A. Yes, sir.

Q. Will you produce that book to the Board?

A. That is a matter I will take into consideration.

Q. The Aldermen have asked what seems a proper question to us; now, we want to know whether you are willing to produce here the items to show what your gas costs?

A. I am an officer of the corporation, and I am in the place of trustee; if my directors, on consultation, are willing I should do it, I will.

Q. We understand that you represent the Boston Gas Gas Light Co.; you are the active man; the president is a capitalist; you are, I believe, the man with whom the citizens, who have occasion to go to the company, come in contact. What I want to know is, if you are willing to give this information?

A. I am willing to give that or any informatien which the Board of Aldermen desire, which does not conflict with the interests of my corporation. That is a matter upon which I will consult my directors, and at the next meeting of the Board make a full statement.

Q. My question is, whether you regard that information as confidential?

A. Whether my directors will give me leave to make the statement at the next meeting of this Board, of course I cannot say.

Q. I do not wish to press you in regard to your private matters, but I suppose, as you are the managing man the directors would do just what you advise them to do in this matter, practically, and what I want to get at is whether you are willing to give us that information.

A. You must remember that you and I have been through this thing once before, and I declined to answer that question.

Mr. Hyde. I represented the city, and I remember very well I could not get any information.

Mr. Greenough. Whether I shall give that information now or not, I want to consider further. At any rate, I will say this. I will come to the next meeting of the Board and give you fully and squarely what I have to say upon that point?

Q. Your corporation started with what capital?
A. $75,000.
Q. Paid in?
A. Paid in.
Q. How much more have you had paid in?
A. Our present capital is $2,500,000; all of which has been paid in.
Q. How much of that was paid in at par?
A. $2,000,000 was paid in at par.
Q. You have recently added half a million to your capital?
A. We have.
Q. You sold that stock at auction?
A. Yes, sir.
Q. How much did that bring, on an average?
A. $727.50 a share, I think.
Q. What was the highest?
A. $735, I think, a few shares sold for.
Q. You have paid regularly dividends of 10%?
A. We have. Yes, sir.

Q. Your works are taxed for what?
A. Our works and real estate are taxed for $3,600,000.
Q. What do you regard as their value?
A. It is impossible to say, sir. Our real estate, which was purchased many years ago, has risen very largely in value; and although it is taxed for this large sum, it is worth no more for our purposes than the sum we gave for it. We suffer in tax on account of the rise in property.
Q. Are you taxed any thing for your pipes in the streets?
A. Yes, sir. They are taxed by law in this State as personal property.
Q. Your stock is taxed directly?
A. No, sir, the stock is not taxed to the stockholders, because the whole property is taxed by the city.
Q. And your pipes are taxed as personal property?
A. Yes, sir.
Q. When you stated the amount as three millions, did you include only the real, or real and personal?
A. I included the whole.
Q, What is the personal?
A. That is $650,000.
Q. What does the $650,000 include?
A. I am unable to say what the city includes in that.
Q. You speak of the personal property and real property. What is included as real estate?
A. The city include, as real estate, all our manufacturing apparatus that is not called personal.
Q. How much gas do you deliver a year now?
A. About six hundred and fifty to seven hundred million feet.
Q. Do you light East Boston?
A. No.
Q. Nor South Boston?
A. No.
Q. Nor Dorchester?
A. No.
Q. Nor Roxbury?

A. No.

Q. Nor Charlestown?

A. No. We light nothing but Boston proper; that is, old Boston, going up to the Roxbury line and Brookline line.

Q. Do you know any city in America, where, on the same territory, there are the same facilities for delivering gas that you have in Boston, where there are so many customers within the same space?

A. O, yes; the city of London.

Q. I say, in America?

A. No; not in America.

Q. Within the territory occupied by your company there are more consumers of gas than are to be found in any other city that you know of?

A. I am not able to speak of the old New York Company — how their territory compares with ours; I should say their streets are more compact than ours.

Q. Are not their streets a great deal wider.

A. Their streets below Canal street are not wider; their territory, I should say, is smaller than ours. Mr. Kennedy can answer that question better than I can; but I should say that New York, below Grand street, is smaller than Boston proper.

Q. You say the gas here is about nineteen-candle power; what has been the average power of gas supplied by your company the past year?

A. I should say about nineteen.

Q. Is it tested by you daily?

A. Yes, sir.

Q. How much does it vary?

A. It varies a candle, more or less?

Q. Does it not ever go as low as fourteen?

A. I never saw it.

Q. As low as sixteen?

A. Possibly; I never saw any as low as sixteen.

Q. How long does it take to make a variation in the gas.

A. That is impossible to say. In order that the Board

may understand that, I will say that all the retorts are charged every four hours, consequently they are divided, and every half hour a certain number are charged. Of course, with the different impulsions of the gas going out through the apparatus, the quality will vary according to the little differences in the coal or heat of the retorts. The gas made in one set of retorts might be a little better or a little poorer than that made in the next set, the same coal being used.

Q. Where do you test it?

A. It is tested at the works. The illuminating power has usually been taken at two places — one at the works and one at the office in West Street. During the last three or four months, it has only been taken at the works, in consequence of the absence of the operator at the office.

Q. How often is it taken?

A. Taken at different hours. It is only taken once a day at each place. But there is a modern appliance in use — the jet photometer — which gives the quality of the gas approximately all the time.

Q. Have you any record at your works to show what amount you have credited out of your earnings to construction account or service account? How much of your earnings, above your dividend of ten per cent, have been expended in any way?

A. That question I cannot answer.

Q. Do your books show?

A. That I cannot tell. I doubt whether the early books of the company are in existence. The books for the last ten or twenty years, I think, would show that.

Q. They would show how much you have earned over and above the dividends you have paid?

A. Yes, sir.

Q. Has it been some millions?

A. No, sir.

Q. Has it been any millions?

A. No, sir.

Q. Has not it been one million?

A. Well, twenty years is a good long time. Twenty years, — fifty thousand a year, over and above our dividends, — I should say I think not.

Q. Are you willing to produce your books to the Aldermen as to that fact?

A. That is a question I should have to refer to my directors; of course we are always happy to give every proper information we can about the company. There is no mystery about our business.

Q. Is there any reason why your company, having had from the citizens of Boston this franchise exclusively in the city proper to supply the city with gas, having had it for all these years, and prevented any person from buying gas of any one else than you, should be unwilling to tell what this article costs which every one uses? I suppose you know, that if you are furnishing it at as low a rate as it could be furnished, it is no object for any one else to come in in competition; but still you have always declined to answer the question?

A. I have never declined but twice, and that was when you have asked me the question.

Q. Haven't you always declined?

A. I don't think I have ever been asked by any one else. If twice constitute always, certainly I have.

Q. Now, why is there any particular reason that you, having this franchise, and furnishing this necessary of life to our people, should decline to answer the question in regard to its cost?

A. Well, there are various reasons which perhaps are more or less binding. The object of the company has been to keep their manufacturing along at an even price, giving the best article they could make to the consumers, and average the price of coal over a series of years. The price of gas depends upon the price of coal, which varies every year, so that it would be necessary to change the price every month in order to make it bear a due proportion to the cost.

Q. Suppose the result of your information should be to

show that you furnish it as cheaply as you can, would not that of itself kill off competition ? Nobody disputes that you manage your business well for yourselves ; but if you should prove by your books that you furnish this article as low as anybody could afford to furnish it, would not that, more than anything else, quiet the feeling in the community that the Gas Company is a monopoly ?

A. I have no doubt that if people had better information, they would be less prejudiced against the Gas Company.

Q. Do you know anybody who could inform them better than you can ?

A. Not about the operation of the Gas Company.

Q. Or about the cost of gas ?

A. No.

Q. Is not the reason you decline to answer because you think, that if you tell what this gas costs, the people would be unwilling longer to purchase it of you at the price you ask ?

A. No, sir.

Q. That has no influence upon you ?

A. Not at all.

Q. And yet you say that if the people had more information on this subject, you think it would cut off competition ?

A. No, sir ; I beg your pardon : I said it would give more satisfaction if they knew more about us ; and they can know more about us if they will take the trouble to ask.

Q. I am taking the trouble to ask, and the two questions about which the people desire information are the quality and the cost.

A. Precisely.

Q. Now, if you are furnishing gas of as good quality, and at a price as cheap as anybody else can furnish it, and the citizens are as well served as anybody else could serve them, I suppose that practically ends the question ; I suppose it ends the discussion which has been going on for twenty years in regard to the Boston Gas Light Company, in which you have spent a great deal of money and a great deal of time, in a variety of ways. Now, if you would give us the information upon this question, I think it would, as the Alderman has said, be more valuable than anything else.

A. I will make this statement, that, in proportion to the cost of our gas, the cost of the material and the value of the gas made, our gas is the cheapest gas made in the United States.

MR. HYDE. I do not think that is an exact answer, because the general impression is that all the gas companies are doing pretty well.

Q. What is your objection to having another gas company?

A. I don't see the necessity of two people doing the work of one; it is precisely the same case as two parallel railroads.

Q. Then, in your judgment, there should be but one railroad in Massachusetts between any two points; between here and New York City, for instance, it is your judgment that one railroad should have the right to do all the business?

A. No, sir. But two parallel railroads, running side by side, would hardly be considered judicious, because they could hardly earn dividends, unless they combined to sell their tickets and transport freight at the same price.

Q. Take Albany and Buffalo: Do you think it would be a good thing for the State of Massachusetts if another railroad could be chartered from Albany to Buffalo, through the Mohawk Valley, to connect with the Boston and Albany at Albany?

A. Of course, two capitals must live where only one capital lived before, and the price at which their tickets are sold, and freight transported, must be such as to enable both companies to live.

Q. I understand all that; those things come in to make up your answer; but I want to know whether, in your judgment, it would not be a good thing for Massachusetts to have another railroad between Albany and Buffalo, connecting with the Boston and Albany, to compete with the New York Central?

A. If it permanently reduced the price of travel between Albany and Buffalo, it would be a good thing.

Q. Don't you think it is a good thing for Boston that the Highland Street Railroad has been chartered?

A. That is a matter I do not know any thing about; whether it has been advantageous or not.

Q. Do you know any injury that has been done to the city of Boston by having the Highland Street Railroad here?

A. I do not know of any injury.

Q. That runs through the same streets, does it not, as the Metropolitan?

A. I really don't know about these railroads; they run in so many directions, and run over so many tracks, and run over one another's tracks so much, that I do not know which is which.

Q. Do you think it is an injury to the city of Boston, that two ice companies may deliver ice in the same streets?

A. No; I should think not.

Q. Is there any reason that applies to this question of competition in the supply of gas, except the inconvenience to the citizens by digging up the streets, that does not apply to every kind of merchandise that is bought and sold in this community?

A. Competing gas companies in the same streets have always been, by common consent over the world (except so far as a new custom has been introduced into some of the cities of the United States recently), considered as a mistake in political economy. You will find in Stuart Mill this whole matter argued out — the impolicy of two rival gas companies in the same streets.

Q. Why is it any more impolitic to have two gas companies, if people will furnish the capital, to supply the citizens with gas, than to have two newspapers; why would you not have one newspaper do all the business?

A. Well, if one newspaper could do the business perfectly well, and have all the items of information, and sell its merchandise at as low a price, I do not know why one paper would not be as good as a dozen.

Q. Do you thing that it is an injury to the city of Boston to have Mr. Hathorne's line of coaches run in the same streets as the Metropolitan horse railroad and the Highland horse-railroad?

A. I do not know that it is.

Q. Don't you think it is an advantage?

A. It seems to be a convenience, certainly, to some people.

Q. Can you tell any reason, except, as I say, the inconvenience caused by taking up the streets, that does not apply to all competition in life? Of course, if you have two stores, there have to be two rents paid; if you build two manufactories of any thing, you have two capitals invested, and so with all kinds of business. Now, do you know any reason that applies to competition in gas that does not apply in the same way to all kinds of business, except the matter of digging up the streets?

A. That is a pretty general question, and requires some reflection. You put in two capitals to do the same business.

Q. You do in all kinds of business. It takes two capitals to do the business of manufacturing, if you have two factories?

A. Yes; but, in all manufacturing business, you have the privilege of selling your produce everywhere. The parallel does not apply to a district where your consumers are numbered; where there are just so many persons to consume the article. If there were two companies which made matches to supply the city of Boston, and they were restricted to that market, and there were just so many consumers of matches and no more, of course those two manufacturers of matches, in order that both of them might live, must agree upon a price at which the matches shall be sold, or one manufacturer must undersell the other, and drive him out of the business.

Q. What I desire to know is just this, — except the matter of digging up the streets, which every one agrees is an inconvenience, and should not be done unless there is an advantage to be derived from it, — is there any more reason why the citizens of Boston should not have their choice as to the company of whom they shall purchase their gas, than that they should not have a choice as to which newspaper they will take, or which street conveyance, or anything else?

A. Of course, if the city of Boston chooses to permit other companies to enter into competition with the Boston Gas Light Company, they have a perfect right to do so.

Q. Now, do you know any reason for opposing that that does not apply to all kinds of competition, except the inconvenience to which I have referred?

A. I don't think you can draw precise parallels in the business; for our business has its own peculiar line. I think I have indicated a peculiarity of the gas business which separates it from almost every other kind of business; that is, that the number of consumers is limited within a certain local space — there are just so many of them. If you have one capital supplying that number, and another capital comes in, it must earn its dividends out of the same number of people, and you produce an unnecessary competition; that is, both corporations must get a living. Suppose you have $2,500,000 put in by the Boston Gas Light Company, which earns ten per cent dividends, and another company comes in and asks to supply the same district with the same amount of capital, then the consumers in the city of Boston have got to pay dividends upon $5,000,000, where before they were paying on $2,500,000.

Q. Supposing the company already existing charges a rate which is more than enough to pay ten per cent on both capitals, then is there not an advantage?

A. If the company with $2,500,000 of capital pays dividends upon $5,000,000, there would seem to be a very good reason for the introduction of another company.

Q. Suppose, instead of allowing your company to go on and increase its capital to five million dollars, another one comes in with a capital of two million five hundred thousand dollars, and we then have the advantage of a low price for gas for a series of years, would that not be better than to have one company do the business, whose price we do not know anything about? There is no more capital, is there?

A. There is no more capital. Your question is in part an argument, and in part a question. If the city of Boston chooses to have five million dollars invested in that way, I have nothing to say about it.

Q. You have no objection?

A. I do not say I have no objection. I should say the work would be done better by one company than two, because they are both monopolies.

Q. Do you think it would be better to have one monopoly than two?

A. I should say, in the case of the gas companies, it would be better to have one monopoly. A single company exercising the privilege of supplying gas to its district, becomes a trustee —

Q. For whom, its stockholders, or the people?

A. Both.

Q. Then, if you are trustee for the people, we should like to know the cost of gas?

A. You return again to that.

Q. I suppose you would not object to answering that question to your directors or stockholders, so far as you are a trustee for them? You stand in a relation of trust to them?

A. Yes, sir.

Q. If you stand in a relation of trustee to the people, why should you not extend to them the same courtesy?

A. Perhaps it may come; I don't know.

Q. Without going over these matters, or asking irrelevant questions, don't you think that, if you had a competing company, it would have a tendency to keep you up to the mark in the manufacture of your article? You have not the stimulus of a competing company to keep you up to that.

A. If it be a stimulus, we have not; but we take as much pains in making our gas to-day as if we had a competing company.

Q. I know; but is it not a general principle, that if there are two competing lines of railroad, for example, it tends to keep both lines up to the mark?

A. Of course, competition sharpens people.

Q. Would not the same thing hold good in the manufacture of gas, — the quality, and all those things?

A. Do you mean the improvements? I do not know that I understand the tendency of that question; it might have a tendency to improve the apparatus.

Q. Does the law remain as it used to be as to your right to collect bills; that is, where a party has occupied a dwelling and has left without paying his gas bill, the next occupant cannot have the gas turned on until he pays the bill of the former tenant?

A. That has never been the law in Massachusetts. The Boston Gas Light Co. never has exercised that power. There has never been any such law in Massachusetss. Philadelphia is the only city where they have exercised that power.

Q. Have you never had it here?

A. No, sir.

Q. What means have you of collecting your bills?

A. The method of collection is this: The bills are given to the appropriate weekly, monthly, and quarterly collectors. They are due in cash when presented. If the monthly bills, which are due the first of the month, are not paid by the twentieth, then a notice is sent to each delinquent, that if the bill is not paid before the twenty-sixth of the month (or allowing five or six days), their gas will be shut off. A certain number of people in town never pay their bills except when the " pincers" come to shut off the gas. With regard to the quarterly customers, our bills are presented as early as possible at the beginning of the quarters, — January, April, July, and October. At the end of the second month in the quarter, if the bills are not paid, a notice is sent out to every delinquent, that his bill is not paid, and must be paid in ten days. If the quarterly consumer does not pay any attention to that, then a cut-off notice is sent, giving him half a dozen days more.

Q. It has never been the practice of the company to shut

off the gas in order to compel people to pay the bills of persons who have occupied the same premises previously.

A. No, sir.

Q. Has your company always been ready to lay pipes in the streets, where the city authorities have wanted them, promptly?

A. As far as I know.

Q. Was not an order introduced into the Legislature last year, by the city, to obtain a law which should authorize the city to compel the company to lay pipes in the streets?

A. That had no reference to Boston proper. There was a bill proposed of that sort, which the committee declined to recommend.

Q. You afterwards laid them, didn't you?

A. That had no reference to us. It had reference to some of the other companies. There has never been any question between the different departments of the city and the Boston Gas Light Company as to where their pipes should be laid.

Q. The manufacture of gas by persons who understand it is no very occult science, is it?

A. It is among the practical sciences. Of course it requires skill and attention ; but there is nothing occult about it, except about the chemistry.

Q. There is no difficulty, if the new company is organized with the proper men, in going on and manufacturing gas. It is not one of the secret sciences?

A. It is not a secret science at all.

Q. (By ALDERMAN HALL). I will ask you whether your corporation could furnish gas to the citizens of Boston at $2.00 per thousand, instead of $2.50, and make a fair per cent of profit on your capital?

A. We could not, at the present price of coal.

Q. (By ALDERMAN WORTHINGTON.) I understand the gentleman to say that he furnishes gas to the citizens for $2.50 per thousand ; will he state to the Board what he furnishes it for to the city of Boston?

A. The public lights are furnished at 2.08\frac{1}{3}$ per thousand feet. Then the city of Boston pays for the gas consumed through meters $2.50 per thousand, with 5 per cent discount; at City Hall, for instance, and at the stations.

Q. (By Mr. HYDE). Is that at a loss?

A. I think it is; at any rate, in a series of years, I should say, there was a loss on the street lights.

Q. Have you ever kept any separate account of that; that is, made up a profit and loss account on the street lights?

A. No, sir; we never have.

Q. (By ALDERMAN CUTTER.) I would like to ask the amount of bills unpaid yearly?

A. That question I cannot answer from recollection; but I will inform the gentleman at the next meeting. I should not dare to state the loss from uncollected bills; it is probably somewhere from half to three-quarters per cent, perhaps more.

Q. (By ALDERMAN PETERS.) How do you get at 2.08\frac{1}{3}$ per thousand for the street lights?

A. When we reduced the price of gas to private consumers, we reduced the price of the street-lamps the same percentage. The price before the reduction, I think, was $2.25; at any rate, whatever it was, when we reduced the price to $2.50 to private consumers, we reduced it for the street-lights the same percentage, and that carried the price down to 2.08\frac{1}{3}$.

Q. Is that supposed to represent, or is it based at all on the cost of the gas to you?

A. Oh, no; it has no relation to the cost. I ought to say this: that in the best regulated gas companies in the world, the price for the street-lamps is the same as to private consumers. Some of the London companies are required by law to charge no more for street-lamps than to private consumers; but when gas companies were first introduced into this country, an exception was made, in order to show the lights in the streets, &c.; and the price of the public lights was put at a discount; and the custom has continued ever since; but, of course, it is open to this objection, that every dollar you deduct from the cost of the street-lights has to be paid by the private consumer.

Q. (By ALDERMAN HALL.) Why should the city be furnished with gas at any less price than its citizens?

A. That is a question I am unable to answer.

Q. (By ALDERMAN PETERS.) Don't you consider it a privilege to be allowed to go through the streets and lay your pipes?

A. It would be a privilege, if it were perpetual.

Q. Don't you consider it perpetual?

A. Well, there is hardly anything in the United States, or anywhere else, that is perpetual; of course, what I mean by that is, that the privilege of taking up the streets is a privilege which we exercise for the consumers of gas, who are supplied by the company.

Q. (By ALDERMAN BROOKS.) I understood you to say that the price of the gas consumed in the public buildings, station-houses, &c., was $2.50 per thousand, with five per cent discount?

A. Yes, sir.

Q. I suppose you make that discount of five per cent on account of the size of the bills?

A. Yes, sir.

Q. How long has it been the custom to take off that five per cent?

A. It began about ten years ago, I should say. It first began with the large private consumers. At first, the rule applied to consumers to the amount of a thousand dollars a year, who paid promptly; a great many of those large consumers did not pay promptly, and so had no right to avail themselves of the five per cent discount; it was limited to those who paid promptly, and it gradually extended to the city.

Q. Do you not at the present time make a deduction to the large consumers?

A. No; only the same deduction that is made to the city.

ALDERMAN HALL. I think it ought to be said here, that while you furnish the gas to the street-lights at what you assume to be about the cost, the city of Boston pays you for the underground work, which private citizens do not pay you for. What is termed the " underground work " cost $13,000 last year.

A. Yes, sir; the underground work belongs to the city.

ALDERMAN HALL. While for the private consumer, who only pays you ten or twelve dollars a year, you run your service pipe from the main inside through the cellar-wall, the city of Boston, which pays you for its street-lights about $125,000 annually, pays you for the underground work a sum amounting to many thousand dollars a year.

A. I think you will find that that custom obtains everywhere. There is one consideration which should be mentioned, and a very important consideration it is: that while the city of Boston is supplied with gas for its street-lights cheaper than any other city, and of a quality quite as good, we suppose, as any gas made in the United States, the city of Boston is considered to be the best-lighted city in the United States.

ALDERMAN HALL. And yet our gas-lights cost us about fifty dollars a lamp; while the city of New York, it seems, has its lights for thirty-three dollars.

A. Of course it would be very improper for me to sit in judgment upon the Chairman of the Committee on Lamps; but I think the gentleman from New York (Mr. Kennedy) said they got two dollars and seventy-five cents per thousand for the gas they supplied to their street-lamps.

ALDERMAN PETERS. And they also do the lighting and extinguishing and cleaning?

A. It is simply a question of figures; any gentleman can, with his pencil, see how much we get per thousand feet. I suppose the gas burns here about as many hours as in New York.

ALDERMAN HALL. They do the lighting and extinguishing and the cleaning; what makes the difference?

A. They supply twenty-five per cent less gas.

Q. (By Alderman Hall.) How do you account for that seventeen dollars' difference?

A. There is a difference of twenty-five per cent to start with. Our lamps burn four feet an hour; theirs burn three.

Q. Do you take into account that their gas is twenty-candle power?

A. Do you suppose the difference of a candle, or a candle and a half, would make any very great difference? What is done to make the difference in price between our gas, as served to the street-lights, and the cost of maintaining a lamp, of course is not within my knowledge.

Q. (By Alderman Brooks.) You say you do not know what makes the difference; but you think it is in the quality of the gas?

A. No, sir; the difference is this. I do not know what it costs to take care of each individual lamp. Alderman Hall states that the cost of each lamp is fifty dollars a year. We know we get so much per thousand feet for the gas we supply. Of course, the question comes up, in comparing the New York lamps with ours, how much gas they supply, and then deduct the price of that from thirty-three dollars, in order to ascertain how much it costs to take care of those lamps. That is a matter of figures simply.

Alderman Peters. I do not think you need to figure at all to see that thiry-three dollars is not as much as fifty dollars.

A. I did not say it was. We are not responsible for the fifty dollars per lamp paid here. We are only responsible for what we charge for the gas supplied to the street-lights. What it costs to take care of the lamps is a matter for the committee.

Q. (By Alderman Hall.) Would you be willing to light the lamps and take care of them at the same rate that they do there?

A. I cannot say whether I would or not, because I do not know what I should have to pay the lighters. Formerly the gas company had charge of the lighting.

Q. I understand that they sell their gas for a quarter of a dollar a foot more than you charge. Now, if they light their lights at thirty-three dollars, clean and take care of them, and still get as much or more per thousand feet than you do, where is that discrepancy?

A. For instance, we deliver four feet an hour, and they deliver three. That is an agreement with the city.

Q. Is it because it takes four feet of your gas to make as good light as three feet of theirs?

A. That, of course, as I have never seen three feet of their gas burning in comparison with ours, I cannot say. Formerly the burners in the street-lights in Boston consumed over four feet an hour; they were the largest in the United States at that time; but it was found, after careful experiments, that four feet an hour would make a sufficient light; and the burners were altered to that size.

J. P. KENNEDY, *recalled.*

Q. (By ALD. WORTHINGTON.) I want to ask you if you think you can construct gas works in the city of Boston, and supply the city and the citizens for two dollars a thousand, and pay a dividend sufficient to maintain the company; make it what would be called a paying stock?

A. It is my impression that I can.

Q. Will you at the next hearing show to the Board of Aldermen the figures showing that, that we may have them to base our votes upon?

A. Well, sir, I will endeavor to do so. It is short notice to figure so much; but I will try to have it, sir.

Q. (By ALDERMAN BROOKS.) I understood you to say (I think I am correct) that the average cost of your gas was $2.75 per thousand feet?

A. The price we sell it at; yes, sir.

Q. And your price for lighting and taking care of the street lamps, $33.00 per lamp, is based on that price for the gas?

A. Yes, sir. It is done in this way. Mr. Greenough

did not answer your question; I presume he did not understand it. The burners in Boston, as I understand it, burn four feet per hour; the burners in New York burn three feet per hour. You see there is a difference in the quantity of gas burned.

Q. Yes; but you say you think you give as good light as we do here?

A. Well, that is my impression, sir; for the reason that the illuminating power of the gas made by the Mutual Company of New York, consumed from a three-foot burner, is equivalent to four feet of ordinary gas.

Q. (By ALDERMAN STEBBINS.) What was the cost of the works of the Mutual Gas Light Company?

A. I think they have spent about three millions and a half.

Q. Your capital stock paid in is two millions and a half?

A. Yes, sir.

Q. And your bonded debt, how much?

A. I think there is about $400,000.

Q. How many years have you been in operation?

A. Between two and three years.

Q. (By ALDERMAN CUTTER). Will you please to state what it costs to take care of a street lamp in New York?

A. We pay thirty cents a month for lighting and extinguishing the lamps, cleaning them, and putting in the glass; if any is broken, the lamp-lighter is required to put that in; but it is provided to him by the city.

The hearing was then adjourned to four o'clock on Monday next.

II.

HEARING

ON

PETITION OF CITIZENS' GAS LIGHT CO.,

NOV. 16 1874.

MONDAY, Nov. 16, 1874.

The hearing was resumed at 4 o'clock.

MR. COLLINS. On last Monday I heard the questions asked by Alderman Worthington, and other Aldermen, about the cost of gas, and the price at which we could make gas for the supply of the citizens of Boston. Mr. Kennedy has been in New York since, and has made some figures. I desire to call him this afternoon to answer some of those questions.

MR. KENNEDY, *recalled*.

Q. (By MR. COLLINS). I want to know if you have, since the last hearing, made any plans or drawings of gas works suitable for the city of Boston, for this company, and estimates of their probable cost?

A. Yes, sir, I have, partially. You are aware that it is something of a piece of work to do. I have approximately done it. I have a set of plans which are very close to what we want here, and I brought them over with me, and have them to exhibit to any committee of the Board who would like to see them.

Q. You are willing to show those drawings, as far as you have made them, to the Board, or any committee of the Board, are you?

A. Yes, sir.

Q. Have you made any estimate of the cost of gas works for the Citizens' Gas Light Co., and also of the cost of laying pipe for the company, to compete with the Boston Gas Light Co.?

A. I haven't made any particular estimates in regard to laying pipe here; it is about the same everywhere.

Q. What do you estimate it would cost to construct the works, and lay the pipe, for the purpose of supplying gas to the gas consumers in the city of Boston by this company?

A. Well, sir, I should put it at about $2,000,000.

Q. Can you go to work for $2,000,000?

A. Yes, sir.

Q. Now, have you made any estimate about the price at which you can furnish gas to the citizens of Boston; in other words, at what price you can manufacture and sell illuminating gas, at a profit, to the citizens of Boston who are now buying gas of the Boston Gas Light Co.?

A. Well, sir, the way that I got that question in my mind from Alderman Worthington, the last time I was here, was this; he wanted to know about the cost of producing gas, and I have to reply to that, that when we have a fair share of the business here, we can manufacture and distribute gas at a cost of about $1.50 a thousand.

Q. What can you furnish that gas to the citizens of Boston for?

A. Well, sir, if we had a consumption say of a million feet a day, on the average, we could sell it for $2.00 per thousand feet.

Q. That is, at the present price of coal?

A. At the present price of coal. Of course, that is a variable article.

Q. What illuminating power would that gas be?

A. Well, sir, from eighteen to twenty candles.

Q. Is the company of which you are the manager in New York, the Mutual Gas Light Co., in competition with the New York, the Manhattan, and the Metropolitan Gas Light Companies?

A. We are, sir.

Q. Is your candle power greater than theirs?

A. It is.

Q. And you furnish it at the same price?

A. Yes, sir; it is two or three times as good.

Q. Your bills are less per month than theirs on account of the richer quality or higher illuminating power of the gas?

A. Yes, sir.

Q. I understand your testimony to be to-day, that gas works, the apparatus, and the pipes for a company to enter into competition with the Boston Gas Light Co. can be furnished at an expense of about $2,000,000; and that, in the second place, gas can be manufactured and sold of a a better quality than is now furnished to the citizens of Boston, by the new company, for about $2 a thousand, provided the consumption is a million feet a day, or three hundred million feet a year?

A. Yes, sir.

Q. Are you aware of the number of feet of gas sold by the Boston Gas Light Company last year?

A. It was stated here at the last meeting as over 700,000,000 feet, I understood.

Q. So that, if you had a chance of selling three-sevenths the amount of gas sold by the Boston Gas Light Company last year, you could sell it for less than one-half the price?

A. Yes, sir.

Q. Perhaps it will be better for me to ask a question which may be asked you from some other source, — are you in any way connected with the Citizens' Gas Light Company of Boston?

A. Well, sir, when I came here first, I came here as an expert, by invitation; and, after I looked over the ground, I concluded to become a stockholder in it.

Q. You came with the expectation, I believe, of competing for the contract to make the works, having had twenty-five years' experience as a gas-works builder?

A. Yes, sir.

Q. I will ask you now whether you are prepared to take stock in this new company; whether you have confidence enough in the ability of this company to furnish gas to the citizens of Boston, and make money by it, to take stock in the company, and, if so, how much?

A. Well, sir, if you will look upon the subscription paper, you will see that I have subscribed for two thousand shares.

Q. And you are willing in good faith to put up that amount of money, if the authority be granted?

A. I am, sir.

Q. Are you willing, as one of the stockholders to the amount of $200,000, to be responsible for a part, one-fifth, say, of a sum to be put up as a forfeit to the city of Boston, or to bind yourselves in any other way that the city of Boston chooses, that this company will go on and build the works, lay the pipes, and furnish gas to those who wish to buy it, and not sell out to any other company?

A. I am, sir, most decidedly.

Cross-Examination.

Q. (By Mr. Morse.) Will, you state the items that go to make up the $2,000,000 which you allow for the cost of the works, &c.?

A. Well, sir, I have stated, as a gas-works builder, what I can do, and I am willing to explain myself in detail to any committee of this Board. I don't know that it is proper for me to stand up here and give the inside of this business publicly.

Q. Do you allow for the cost of land when you say that the entire expense will be $2,000,000?

A. Of course I do, sir.

Q. How much do you allow for that?

A. Well, sir, I have only to reply to that, that I am here in the interest or behalf of the Citizens' Gas Light Company. I am not here to tell the Boston Gas Light Company what I can do. They haven't employed me for that purpose.

Q. That answer was first suggested to you by counsel, was it not?

A. No, sir, I suggested to counsel whether I should make that answer.

Q. You decline to state what you allow for the cost of land?

A. I do, sir, in this way. I say again, I repeat it, that to a committee of this Board of Aldermen, I am ready to give all the particulars, all the figures, but I beg to decline to give them to you. You are not a stockholder in this company, and the business of this company belongs to the stockholders exclusively, according to my views of business.

Q. I am not asking these questions in behalf of the Boston Gas Light Company. I am asking them for the benefit of the Board who are to hear and determine this question.

A. I am ready to respond to the Board in a proper way.

Q. How much land do you allow for?

A. Well, sir, we should require several acres.

Q. How many acres?

A. Well, I don't think that is important, sir, if the company have the money to purchase them. They will get anywhere from three to ten, if they require it.

Q. Would three acres be sufficient?

A. Well, I don't think it would be quite enough, sir.

Q. How many would be sufficient?

A. Well, I can't see the object of your inquiry, sir. I can't see how it throws any light upon this subject.

Q. Would five acres be sufficient?

A. Well, that I will determine when I make the ground plan of the works. I haven't done it yet. I never do that until I see the land.

Q. Well, how many acres did you include in your two million dollars?

A. Well, sir, I am not prepared to answer that.

Q. Did you make any allowance for any specific number of acres?

A. Why, as a matter of course, I did.

Q. Can you state what it was?

A. I can, but I decline to do it.

Q. What reason have you for declining?

A. Because I don't think, if you will pardon me for the expression, that it is any of your business.

Q. You come here prepared to make a statement in answer to the question of one of the Aldermen what would probably be the cost of the works of the new company?

A. I beg leave to say that I have been for twenty-five years doing this business. I have executed some of the largest contracts in the United States, and I know just exactly what I am about all the time. When parties employ me, I know just how to advise them. I want to say that for your information.

Q. I am much obliged to you for the information, but it don't help us along at all. Are you acquainted with the value of land in Boston?

A. I think I am, sir. I have been posted about that.

Q. How long have you been in Boston?

A. I have been here off and on; I can't say exactly how many hours, or days, or weeks.

Q. How many hours do you think you have been in Boston?

A. Well, sir, I have been here long enough to know what the price of land is. I beg to assure you of that.

Q. Well, what is the price of the land that you allowed for these works? How much do you allow a foot or an acre for it?

A. Well, land runs all the way from fifty cents to two dollars a foot here.

Q. Is two dollars the maximum?

A. I don't know that.

Q. Without going now to the question of the quantity of land, how much a foot or an acre do you allow for the land you propose to take?

A. That I will reply to my board of directors when they ask me the question.

Q. You don't propose to tell anybody else?

A. I propose, as I said before, — I wish to state it distinctly, — if there is a committee of the Board who want every detail of this thing, I am at liberty to give it.

Q. Will you answer it now if one of the Aldermen will ask the question?

A. No, sir, I beg leave to decline. I will answer to a committee of the Board. I don't see the object of the request.

Q. Then, as I understand you, you don't decline to answer because I ask the question, but you would decline to answer anybody here?

A. Well, sir, I have just stated what I propose to do. I am willing to give the Board any information they want, or a committee of the Board, but I don't see the propriety of my going into these details here, for the benefit of other people who have no interest in it, beyond the Board of Aldermen.

Q. What buildings do you include in your estimate?

A. Well, sir, you know the buildings that are incident to gas works; retort house, purifying house, officers' house, coal house, valve house, gas-holder, tank,— all those articles that are incident to gas works.

Q. What do you allow for the cost of those buildings?

A. I decline to answer that, sir. I decline to answer any thing touching that.

Q. How many gas-holders have you allowed for?

A. I decline to answer that also. I don't think that enters into the question at all.

Q. How many miles of street mains have you allowed for?

A. Enough to accommodate the city.

Q. How many?

A. Well, I don't propose to tell you that, sir.

Q. Have you formed an estimate in your own mind how many miles of street main will be needed to acommodate the city?

A. Yes, sir, I have.

Q. How many is it?

A. Well, sir, I don't know what that has to do with the subject matter, at all.

Q. You decline to state to the Board how many miles of street main you have allowed for?

A. I don't decline to state to the Board, but I decline to state it to you, most decidedly.

Q. I don't ask you to state it to me; but will you state to the Board how many miles of street mains in your judgment are necessary to supply the city of Boston with gas?

Mr. COLLINS. I object to that question, and I will state here that we do not propose to give the Boston Gas Light Company any information that our stockholders alone should have. We do not propose to tell publicly, in the hearing of the Boston Gas Light Company and others, just how much it is going to cost to construct the works to supply the citizens of Boston, who are now supplied by the Boston Gas Light Company. We propose to tell them how much we can manufacture and sell the gas for. We do not propose to tell our private business to the Boston Gas Light Company, or to its agents or attorneys, or to tell our private business to the Board of Aldermen in the presence of the agents of the Boston Gas Light Company. They may ask the information from now until ten o'clock, and they will not get it. As Mr. Greenough says, that is information which belongs to the company. You will get in round numbers what we can do, but you shall not have the details.

Mr. MORSE. It is, of course, for the Board, and not for the counsel, to determine how far this investigation shall go. Our position here is simply this: At the proper time, we shall, of course, have to state the reasons why we believe that it is not for the interest of the city to permit the introduction of the pipes of this company as proposed. But for the present, we simply submit to the Board that when this company comes in here, and asks for permission to dig up the streets of the city without any limitation as to boundary lines, not asking to go into this or that part of the city, but into all parts of the city, it must beforehand give to the Board reasonable satisfaction, first, that it has the means to carry out the plan that it intends; and, secondly, that the carrying out of those plans will result in a reduction of the price of gas to the citizens of Boston. I need not say that there are a good many considerations which would influence parties to come here and get permission from this Board to lay down pipes, which are not *bona fide*, so far as the intention to supply the city of Boston with gas at a less price is concerned; and it is for this Board to test the good faith and ability of the parties who come before them.

Of course, Mr. Chairman, as companies, we have no right here. It is only by your favor that we stand here permitted to put questions for the purpose of testing the correctness of the judgment of the witnesses. We stand here, as it were, in your place, or as your assistants. We have no power to judge. We have nothing to do here, except to be of service, if we can be, in testing the correctness of the opinions, and the truth of the facts, that are stated by the witnesses. If we go one inch beyond what you think to be the true line of professional duty in putting questions, if we put any question which in your judgment is intended in any way to embarrass or harass a witness, then, of course, we should be checked, and we are quite willing to be, and abide by your judgment; but if we are seeking, in good faith, to put questions for the purpose of probing this whole matter to the bottom, bringing out what are the facts that lie beneath this whole application, and to show what is the power of these gentlemen to carry out their plan, how much consideration they have given to the subject, what will be the probable result of this experiment on their part, — I say, if we proceed in good faith in behalf of the companies which we respectively represent, we ask to be permitted to go on as we have begun. I reminded the Board at the former hearing, that this is a question not to be disposed of hastily. Here are corporations that for the larger part of half a century have supplied the city of Boston and adjacent towns or cities with gas. It is now proposed that the policy of the city shall be changed, and that a competing corporation should be allowed to come into the same streets, to occupy them, and lay down their pipes. It is a question of very grave importance, one that is not to be disposed of hastily. It is not to be voted upon in an hour or an evening. It is one which involves the fullest inquiry; and if the suggestion of the learned counsel on the other side should be followed, to which we do not object, that this Board shall appoint a committee who shall examine the question carefully and in detail, we are perfectly willing that the matter should be investigated in that way; but we submit to the Board, that, if this matter is to be considered in these public sessions, we should have the privilege of putting questions that are put in good faith; and, as I said before, if we ask a single question that is not put in that way, I trust we shall be checked. But if this investigation is to go on here, we ask the privilege of putting these questions in good faith for the purpose of testing not merely the good faith of the parties, but testing the accuracy of their judgment, and the extent to which they have considered the essential questions that must be determined by them before giving information that will be of any value to this Board.

MR. COLLINS. It is true that this is a question that is not to be decided hastily, and if the interest of the Boston Gas Light Co. is consulted, the question will never be decided. That is precisely what the company desires. Their policy is procrastination. If they can put it off a year, it is well. If they can put it off three years, it is better. If they can put it off for all eternity, it is a great deal better still. It is a question that deserves to be well considered, but it is one that must be decided. It is not a question that is to be turned aside by quibbles. The learned counsel has told us just what the questions are here; first, have this company the capital to carry out their intentions? secondly, can they supply the citizens of Boston with a better quality of gas, at a cheaper rate than the Boston Gas Light Co? It is of no concern to the Board of Aldermen how many tanks there will be, how many miles of pipe, how many gas holders, how many retorts, how much the land is to cost, whether two dollars a foot, or fifty cents a foot. It is, if I may be pardoned for saying it, none of the business of the Boston Gas Light Co. how much a foot the land is going to cost, if the company have the money to buy it. If they desire to test the accuracy of the witness now on the stand, they may impeach him if they please. He has testified that he has built more gas works than any other man in this country. His experience is the largest. He comes on the stand and says he has estimated how much it would cost to build the works, and furnish the requisite apparatus, and that it will cost $2,000,000. Then he goes on and says that, supplying 300,000,000 feet per year to the citizens, the gas can be made at $1.50 a thousand feet and supplied at $2. To go beyond that, to inquire into particular details which belong to the directors of the company, is something which I say the Boston Gas Light Co. has no business to do. I say here, that our plans, our estimates, and all the details, if necessary, shall be submitted to the Board of Aldermen, or to any committee of the Board, but not for the information of the Boston Gas Light Co. The Board are to be satisfied of our good faith by our subscription list, by the money that is here, and by the forfeit which we propose to give to the city of Boston, who may put all the checks, guards, and limits upon us they choose. 1 submit that we are met by just one remonstrant, and that is the monopolist that has had the entire charge of delivering gas to the people of Boston for more than fifty years; and, if they are coming here in the interest of the public, it is an entirely new guise that they are assuming. I submit it is one corporation against another, and it is not for the counsel to come here and say that he is going to probe this matter to the bottom in good faith. He is looking out for the interest of his private concern. The Board of Aldermen, representing the public, may have all the information they desire to satisfy them that our corporation can go on and carry out their plans; but we do not propose to lay open the private concerns, the minutiæ and details of our corporation, to the counsel who represents the Boston Gas Light Co., or any other company that we desire to compete with; we do not think that we should be required to do so; but to the Board of Aldermen, or to any committee thereof, we will give the fullest details, the smallest minutiæ of our business, in confidence.

MR. FIELD. I appear for the Roxbury Gas Light Company; and, if I may be permitted, I should like to say one word at this time. The testimony of this witness is, that with an expenditure of $2,000,000 for plant, the company can manufacture gas for $1.50 per thousand feet, and sell it for $2.00. His testimony has been that the corporation which he represents proposes to make just this plant, and to do just this thing. He is an expert in gas, but he has given his estimate in gross.

Now, it never was heard of before any tribunal under heaven, that a man called to give his opinion upon what can be done in a hypothetical case, or explain how much money will turn out what result, — it was never heard of anywhere, that that witness was not to give the details of his hypothesis, or the details of his supposition, how he makes it out. He has not undertaken to give what they propose to do; but he has stated that, upon the expenditure of so much money, gas can be manufactured at such a rate. He puts it in gross; and, in such a case, it was never heard of before in any tribunal in the world, that the witness was not to be examined to show whether his statement is conjecture, or made upon knowledge. It does concern every citizen of Boston whether gas can be made permanently, at this price, for the whole city and suburbs; but, under every rule that governs the introduction of testimony anywhere, hypothetical testimony like this must be either withdrawn altogether, or the grounds upon which it is made up must be given.

MR. COLLINS. If the counsel had been present at the last meeting, he would have known that this statement is connected with another statement made then. Mr. Kennedy came on the stand, and said that the new corporation could furnish the people of Boston with better gas at a less price per thousand, and at a less cost in the manufacture, than the gas now furnished by the Boston Gas Light Company. Alderman Worthington and some other gentlemen desired the figures. Mr. Kennedy had not made any at that time. He comes now, and says it can be done. Now, you must connect our offer to-day with the statement of our ability to do it. We have put on a gas engineer of twenty-five years' experience who tells you it can be done. Now, if the Boston Gas Light Company desires to know how to make gas at $1.50 per thousand feet, and sell it at $2.00 per thousand feet, they have got to employ him and pay him. We do not propose to give the details here.

ALDERMAN POWER. I suppose this Board desires to get all the information that can be got on this very important subject. Now, as a member of this Board, I should desire to have the representatives of this new company show all the details of this business, and how they are going to be able to offer to furnish gas for less than the Boston Gas Light Company; but, if they are obliged to do this, I want to know from the other side, as there appear to be only two sides to this question, the Boston Gas Light Company and the Citizens' Gas Light Company, I want the Boston Gas Light Company to show from their books and accounts for the last twenty-five years why it cannot be done, so that this Board may have both sides. That is the only way we can get at it. Mr.

Greenough, on behalf of the other company, said that certain information asked for here was the property of his directors. Now, I think that the proposition which this company make here cannot be gainsaid unless they show us the contrary, and it is within their power to give us the facts on the subject. If they will agree to do that, I should hope that this company would be obliged to give us the fullest details as to how they propose to make gas cheaper.

MR. MORSE. In answer to the suggestion made by one of the Aldermen just now, I desire to say this, that if, after the investigation has been made into the condition and the estimates of this new organization, it should be, in the judgment of the Board, material or proper to inquire into the details of the cost of the manufacture by the Boston Gas Light Company, or of any other of the gas companies here, I understand that no objection will be interposed to their being furnished. I do not understand that there has ever been any other objection than this, that at some hearing that took place some years ago, the matter was brought up under such circumstances that the officer of the corporation then present did not feel justified in exhibiting the books of the company which were asked for. The other night, the question was put when he was in no position to make a reply; but without stating in detail precisely what can be furnished or will be furnished, I am justified in saying to the Board, that there will be no reluctance on the part of the officers of the company to answer any inquiries that in the judgment of the Board should seem proper in respect to the manufacture of gas, only I wish to be understood that it may not be necessary to go into that, if the Board shall be of opinion, upon the examination of these gentlemen, that they themselves cannot show a manufacture for any less than that by the Boston Gas Light Company. The Board will perceive that now the utmost difference that is made is fifty cents a thousand feet. The gentleman has stated, that in his judgment it can be made so as to be sold for $2.00 instead of $2.50. That is the entire difference that is now pretended, and as I said before, when the examination of their experts is finished, the Board may not think that they have shown that it can be made for less than $2.00, so as to be sold for less than $2.50.

MR. PUTNAM. If the Board will permit a single word, I have before stated, that I represent one of the gas companies of the city (the South Boston Gas Light Company), and I have been at several hearings at which similar questions to this have been raised. I wish to call the attention of the Board to the fact, that the class of questions which Mr. Kennedy has refused to answer to the counsel of the Boston Gas Light Company, is one to which, so far as I can remember, answers have never been refused at previous hearings. The agent of the Boston Gas Light Company, and the agents of other gas companies, so far as questions have been put to them, have refused to disclose exactly what it cost them to make their gas, that being a question depending upon a great many elements which change from day to day, and from year to year, which vary with the course of trade, and which, if disclosed, would amount to a disclosure of their business, not merely as gas furnishers, but as merchants, buying coal, and making it into a product and selling it. I never heard an agent of a gas company refuse to tell what it cost per mile to lay pipes, or what land costs in the city of Boston, or what it would cost to build a retort house, or to make gas holders. On the contrary, I do not understand that information of that class was ever refused on the ground that it was a trade secret. When, therefore, the witness and his counsel refuse to answer questions of the character which have been put, questions simply going into the details of an estimate given in gross, as to the cost of laying pipes throughout the city, and undertake to shelter themselves behind the privilege of trade secret, they undertake to do what has never been done before, I believe, in all the hearings of this kind, and something which was never undertaken, I think, before any tribunal where it became important to ascertain the reliability of estimates given in gross.

Q. (By MR. MORSE.) I will repeat the question. You decline to state to the Board how many miles of street-main will be needed to accommodate the city?

MR. COLLINS. I will state that the witness will refuse to give any details to the counsel of the Boston Gas Light Company; but any information, however minute, relating to the construction of the works, or the internal affairs of the company, will be given to this Board, or to any committee of the Board.

THE CHAIRMAN. The petitioners have stated here that they can put up gas works to supply the citizens with gas, at an expenditure of $2,000,000. The remonstrants doubt that, evidently. The Chair would decide, unless overruled by the Board, that it is perfectly competent and desirable that Mr. Kennedy should answer the questions in regard to his estimates for the construction of these works; such, for instance, as the amount that will be required for land, for the laying of the main-pipes, &c. Any secrets which they may have in regard to the manufacture of gas, whether they can produce a better quality, or produce it at a less price, than the Boston Gas Light Company, or any other gas light company, is something which they are not called upon to expose at the present time. But it does seem to the Chair, that it is very proper that he should answer questions in regard to what amount will be necessary for the purchase of land, for the laying of main-pipes, &c. The petitioners have shown here that the works can be constructed for $2,000,000. If it can be shown, on the contrary, that it will cost more than $2,000,000 to purchase the land and erect the buildings, it is very evident that gas works cannot be put in working operation for $2,000,-000. The Board of Aldermen are desirous, as I understand, to learn as much as possible at this hearing, and rather a wide latitude will be given to both sides.

Mr. Collins. We have stated that the works can be built and the pipe laid, the meters and other apparatus furnished, for $2,000,000, and gas supplied for $2.00 per thousand feet. We go no further. If the remonstrants show that it cannot be done, it will be time for us to rebut it by details.

Mr. Morse. I suppose the burden is upon the petitioners to make out their case originally.

Mr. Collins. We do not say the whole city of Boston can be piped for that amount. We say the territory over which the Boston Gas Light Company extends. The witness will answer the question about the number of miles of pipe, and what it will cost per mile.

The Witness. It will be impossible for me to tell the exact number of miles of pipe.

Q. (By Mr. Morse.) That is not the question. You have given an estimate that it would cost $2,000,000 to buy the necessary land, put up the necessary buildings, and lay the necessary pipes. Now, my question, for the purpose of testing the correctness of that estimate, is, what amount did you allow for street-mains?

A. I allowed for laying one hundred miles of street-main to begin with.

Q. At how much per mile?

A. The price of street mains would vary from $3,000 to $30,000 a mile.

Q. It would make a good deal of difference whether you allowed $3,000 or $30,000 a mile for the expense of laying the mains. I should like to know what you allowed.

Mr. Collins. You cannot know. You may sit here until ten o'clock, and you cannot know.

Mr. Morse. I am not asking you, but the witness.

Mr. Collins. The witness will do pretty much as I say about that.

Mr. Putnam. You have got him in good training, I see.

Q. (By Mr. Morse.) Did you make a specific estimate of the cost per mile for the street mains?

A. Yes, sir.

Q. What was it?

A. Well, sir, I can only repeat what I said before, I decline to answer.

Q. How much did you allow for the land, or rather, I will go back of that, how much land did you allow for?

A. My estimate for the works, and one hundred miles of pipe was $2,000,000 in round numbers. I was here on last Monday evening, and I couldn't go into the details to a penny since then; but on my general knowledge of my business, and my reflection since, I have made that estimate.

Q. Have you made any estimate at all in detail?

A. I have, sir. What is, "in detail"? I said just a moment ago it would be impossible to do it to a penny since last Monday evening, but I have in a general way.

Q. Now, in a general way, will you state how much of that $2,000,000, you allowed for land, and buildings, and how much for pipes?

A. I don't think that enters into the question at all.

Q. Have you made the estimate in detail under those three heads, — land, buildings, and pipes?

A. I have made a general estimate; yes, sir.

Q. Have you made an estimate of those three items separately?

A. Of course I couldn't make any estimate of the whole without I took it in detail in that way.

Q. You decline to state how much you allowed for the buildings, and land, and pipes?

A. I do sir. I decline most decidedly.

Q. Or how much land you allowed for?

A. Yes, sir.

Q. And how much for buildings?

A. Yes, sir. I stated the buildings a short time ago.

Q. How large buildings?

A. That is a matter I will tell my Board when I make the ground plan.

Q. How large a population did you estimate to supply when you speak of the entire cost being $2,000,000?

A. Well, I think every gentleman would have an idea how many people would be reached by a hundred miles of pipe, just as well as I can tell them.

Q. It would depend something on where they started from, and through how many of the smaller streets they were laid, wouldn't it?

A. Yes, sir.

Q. What portion of the city did you estimate for?

A. Well, sir, we didn't go out on the vacant part of the city, where the vacant lots are.

Q. Did you estimate to put your works in the city or out of the city?

A. We have three or four locations in view, but haven't decided upon any one of them yet. We haven't purchased our land yet, because we are hardly in a condition to do it.

Q. That was not my question. I don't ask for any secrets of this company, but I want to know how much land you estimated for?

A. Well, I am not going to tell that, sir — how much land. I have declined that several times, Mr. Morse. We shall probably want from five to ten acres. I can't tell.

MR. MORSE. I submit to the Chairman whether or not the question how much land they allowed for is a proper question.

THE CHAIRMAN. The Chair would state that, in his opinion, it is a proper question. It is proper for him to answer how much land he has estimated for in the construction of these works, which can be built for two million dollars. If he says that it is one acre, if the Boston Gas Light Company can show to the satisfaction of this Board that it will require five acres, it will show to the Board conclusively that he has been mistaken in his estimates.

ALDERMAN POWER. It appears to me that the time of this Board and the time of the public can be saved, and that this whole thing can be ascertained and brought to a close in one way quicker than any other. The Boston Gas Light Company has supplied the city of Boston with gas fifty years. I presume it has, to a great extent, the confidence of the people; that they believe it will do what it agrees to do. We know the Boston Gas Light Company. We know the representatives of it; and they can show to this Board, in a very short time, what it costs to furnish gas; and if they show it to this Board, I think the Board will take their word, or their accounts. If that company show that neither they, nor any other company can afford to furnish gas for what the new company claim that they will be able to furnish it, that will end this whole thing. Mr. Kennedy comes here from New York. He is a stranger to all of us; he is an expert, and has carried on this business of putting in gas-works. He states from his experience that he can put in gas-works here to supply a certain number of feet of gas per year for a certain sum of money. If he has got to stop and prove every thing, it appears to me it is going to take a great length of time. The Boston Gas Light Company can show us just what it costs to make gas; and I think this Board is willing to take their statement, if they will give it; and that will end this whole subject, and save a great deal of time to all parties. It appears to me that that is the shortest way to settle this question.

MR. MORSE. I appreciate entirely the motives of the Alderman who has just spoken; and I thank him for the manner in which he has expressed the confidence of the Aldermen in these companies; yet, at the same time, I think a single word of explanation will show that the mode which he suggests would not be the proper mode to take here. Of course, it is a matter of familiar knowledge, that every few years, or every few months, somebody desires an investigation, or petitions the city government for a hearing in reference to a plan for the city to manufacture gas, or for some other company to lay down its pipes, and manufacture gas. If it were understood that all the petitioner need to do was to come in with his petition, to present it to the Board, and say, "There is my petition. I am ready to dig up the streets, lay down pipes, and furnish gas at a less price than the Boston Gas Light Company does," and then impose upon the company the burden of coming here and producing its accounts, or showing from testimony the condition of the company, and the cost of the manufacture of gas, and the amount of profit that it makes, it would be extremely unfair to the company. It would open a way for a great many people to make expense and trouble to the company, as well as annoyance to the city government. Now, there is but one rule, I submit, to be applied to all these cases; and that is the one which in every case you have applied. Where a petitioner comes in and asks that the policy of the city may be changed, he must go forward and prove, in the first place, something tending to support his petition. If he does, and then the party who comes here remonstrating against his petition fails to meet his allegations, of course the petitioner makes out his case; but it would not be a good principle here, any more than it would be in a court of law, to say that a petitioner could come in, throw down his petition, and call upon the remonstrants to put in their case. As I said before to my friend the Alderman, who has just spoken, I do not believe the Board will find any improper reluctance upon the part of the officers of the gas companies represented here to furnish any information which the Board may desire; but I do think that we have a right, in the first place, to have the petitioners exhaust their case. We do not want their case coming in piece-meal. After the case for the remonstrants has been submitted, they may discover and put in further testimony. We want to know it all now. We want to know how much attention they have given to this subject, how far they have gone, what they have ascertained, what they can show to this Board : and then, if after we have investigated that, the Board shall desire to hear from us, of course we are ready to put in our case.

ALDERMAN POWER. I think it is well enough to get all the information we can upon this subject; but I think, when a party comes in here and petitions for a certain thing, we must infer, when responsible gentlemen come forward and say that they have a certain amount of capital, and propose to do a certain thing, that they are acting in good faith; and it seems to me it is for those who oppose that petition to show why they oppose it. That is the way it seems to me. They have come in here and ask that they may have a certain privilege; they state why they want it; they state what they can do. A man of experience comes here and says what he can do. It appears to me it is for any one who opposes the petition to show that it cannot be done.

ALDERMAN WORTHINGTON. I agree fully with the Alderman that we want an answer to these questions; but how can they be answered before they are put? First, state your case, and then have your answer. The case has not been stated. We have had the broad assumption that a certain thing can be done. The Alderman does not allow a man to come before the committee on sewers and say, " I want a sewer in such a street." He requires him to state why he wants it, and give all the facts, so that he will be able to present them to this Board if they are asked for. I do not see how the gas companies who remonstrate against this petition can answer any thing until it is presented. I certainly cannot understand their answer until I know what they are answering.

MR. COLLINS. It seems to me that it does not tend to throw any light upon this question, as to how much it costs to manufacture gas, to find out how many acres of land will be used, or to find out where it is proposed to buy them, if this company has got money enough to buy four or five acres somewhere in the city of Boston. I would like to know of what consequence it is to the Aldermen how many they buy, if they have got the money to pay for it. I beg the Aldermen to keep their eyes upon the main question, and that is, the ability of this company to do what they say they are willing to do ; and also to supply the people of Boston with an article which they say they are perfectly ready to make.

ALDERMAN WORTHINGTON. When the petitioners came before us last week, they told us that this meant business. Now, sir, we want to know all the particulars. We want to know whether it means business. We want them to state how much they can do for $2,000,000. I am told that the Boston Gas Light Company have $7,000,000 invested in this work, and this new company comes here and makes the broad assertion that for $2,000,000 they can put up works and supply gas to the city of Boston. I want to go into the particulars of that thing. If it means business, it means business right through, and they must state directly and squarely how they are going to bring it within the $2,000,000 ; otherwise, I shall not be satisfied, and I do not believe any member of this Board will be satisfied. I am in favor of giving the citizens of Boston cheap gas. If it can be furnished for two dollars a thousand feet, I am in favor of getting it; but I am not in favor of breaking up our streets, and putting the city to the expense of two or three hundred thousand dollars for repair of streets, and all the trouble we shall have through the city, and then find, after all, $2,000,000 will not be more than one-half or one-third the amount that will be necessary to furnish the city. If it can be done, I want it shown here how it can be done.

MR. COLLINS. It does not cost the city any thing.

ALDERMAN BROOKS. It seems to me that the evidence which is called for is perfectly competent. I asked the question the other evening, how much money had actually been paid in by the Boston Gas Light Company, and the representatives of that corporation answered two and a half millions. Now, they started, if I understand it, with $75,000 capital. I don't know how we are going to get at this, unless we allow evidence to be put in here. If the Boston Gas Light Company have not paid in, up to the present time, but two and a half millions, and these people undertake to start with $2,000,000, what will we reckon that corporation worth to-day? They say they have not actually paid so much in dividends. Well, if they have paid ten per cent dividends, or about fifty per cent of their entire capital stock, then it is clearly shown that the Boston Gas Light Company have made money both ways, both upon their gas, and upon the property they have put into the hands of the corporation, and they have charged the people for the full price, while they have put into the corporation double the interest they have paid out.

Mr. KENNEDY. Mr. Alderman Worthington, I would like to explain the matter you spoke of when you were up. This company, sir, does not propose, at the commencement, to pipe the entire city of Boston. It would be preposterous to attempt it with that amount of money; but I said I could give them a hundred miles of pipe, and add to them as our business prospered. That is the proper way for parties to go into business. We do not propose to pipe every street, lane, and alley in the city of Boston, as these gentlemen understand, at the first comencement. We propose, as our business increases, to add to our pipes by degrees.

Q. (By Mr. MORSE.) Are you willing to answer the question which I put a little while ago, as to how much land you have estimated for?

A. Mr. Morse, you know that it would take about five acres of land to put up works of that size.

Q. (By THE CHAIRMAN.) Did you estimate, Mr. Kennedy, for five acres?

A. Yes, sir, I did.

Q. (By Mr. MORSE.) Five acres of land and a hundred miles of pipe?

A. Yes, sir.

Q. Now, are you not willing to state what you allowed for the cost of the five acres?

A. I will tell you how I figured. In round numbers, I figured for the land and plant one million dollars, and for the pipes and services another million. We would have to put the services in for nothing, and to set the meters without cost to the consumers. I believe the service-pipe is generally charged to people, but having paid for those, we could not ask them to pay again for them. That is about the way I figured it, sir.

Q. That is the entire detail that you made?

A. Yes, sir.

Q. Now, in regard to the cost of the gas, did you estimate on the assumption that naphtha was to be used, or not?

A. No, sir.

Q. Do you use naphtha at your works in New York?

A. We do for illuminating our gas. We use it in lieu of Cannel Coal.

Q. In your gas in New York you use naphtha entirely, instead of high priced Cannel Coal?

A. Yes, sir: our gas is made of the ordinary American coals; and, instead of using Cannel Coal to illuminate it, we use naphtha.

Q. What is the highest priced coal you use in New York?

A. Well, sir, coal costs us, this year, about $7.75.

Q. That is the average, is it?

A. That is about the average.

Q. You use no Cannel Coal of any description?

A. No, sir.

Q. Well, what is the highest priced coal you use?

A. Well, sir, we don't use any higher priced coal than that; we have used some Ritchie Mineral at times, but do not use it now.

Q. You make a saving by using naphtha, don't you?

A. Yes, sir, we make a saving for the company, and a saving for the people.

Q. What quantity of naphtha do you use to a ton of coal?

A. Some twenty-five or thirty per cent of the quantity of gas we make, we make from naphtha.

Q. What quantity of naphtha do you keep on hand?

A. Our storage varies: sometimes we have a thousand barrels, sometimes we have ten thousand. We keep it in an iron tank.

Q. Where is the iron tank?

A. The tank is on the premises.

Q. On which side of the city is it?

A. On the east side, foot of Twelfth St.

Q. It is in the river?

A. No, sir, it is on the wharf. It is in our yard.

Q. You have had an explosion of naphtha there, haven't you?

A. No, sir: never.

Q. Hasn't there been an explosion of naphtha in New York?

A. Not in our works.

Q. Hasn't there been any explosion?

A. There has been in the refineries, not in the gas works.

Q. Of naphtha?

A. No, sir; petroleum. That is incident to petroleum refineries; they will blow up sometimes; but we do not handle our stuff in the same way, so we have no trouble.

Q. Is it not a fact, that you and your associates have talked over the plan of substituting naphtha for the high priced coal?

A. No, sir.

Q. Have not you and your associates talked about it?

A. It has been talked about, but we abandoned the idea.

Q. Why?

A. We stated, in the first instance, that we are going to build coal works, and we still adhere to that.

Q. Why did you abandon naphtha here, if you used it in New York?

A. Well, sir, I am not dictator, I am only the engineer of this company.

Q. Do you approve of abandoning the idea?

A. Well, I do not, myself, personally.

Q. Then you are in favor of using naphtha?

A. I would be. Yes, sir.

Q. Then, if you had your way in regard to the management of this company, you would use naphtha, wouldn't you?

A. As I do not expect to have my own way, I do not say.

Q. That does not answer my question. I ask you, whether, if you had your own way, you would not use naphtha?

A. Of course, sir; a man will always back up his opinion.

Q. You propose to own two thousand shares of the stock of this company?

A. I do; yes, sir.

Q. And pay for it in what, in constructing the works?

A. Now, I do not know as that is any of your business.

Q. I mean to ask you a proper question.

A. I have the money to pay for it.

Q. You don't propose to pay any money, do you?

A. I do; yes, sir. I have not thought of that.

Q. Has not this plan of your buying these shares been suggested in connection with your building these works?

A. Certainly it has. That is the object: I am a gas-works builder.

Q. You have never proposed to take this stock independently of building the works, have you?

A. Certainly not.

Q. You are the only person, who has had practically to do with the manufacture of gas, who is connected with the organization, are you not?

A. Well, sir, I suppose, practically, I am; but there are parties connected with me who are gas-stock owners.

Q. You said it had been determined not to use naphtha; when was it so determined?

A. I said we had talked about the matter. It has been mere talk, sir.

Q. I thought you said it had been determined not to use naphtha?

A. I said we had talked about it. I do not know that it has or has not. I cannot say as to that. I do not know what you are trying to get at, sir. If you are trying to provoke me, I do not think you will make much at it; but I do like to be treated like a gentleman; I don't want to be treated as though I was in the criminal court.

MR. MORSE. I do not think I have done that.

WITNESS. I think you are coming at me in just that way.

Q. I will put the question again. Has or has it not been determined to use naphtha?

A. It has not been determined to use naphtha.

Q. Has it been determined not to use it?

A. Yes, sir.

Q. Won't you give the grounds of your opinion that gas can be made from coal for $1.50 per thousand feet, superior to the quality of the gas of the Boston Gas Light Company?

A. I cannot state the grounds, except from my experience as a gas maker.

Q. Have you ever made gas for $1.50 per thousand feet from coal?

A. I have.

Q. Where?

A. Oh, several places.

Q. Where, for one?

A. Well, I have done it in New York, and I have done it in San Francisco.

Q. In what company in New York?

A. I did it in the Metropolitan Company.
Q. When?
A. In 1863.
Q. (By ALD. STEBBINS.) What was the price of coal at that time?
A. It was very similar to what it is now: 1 think about the same price: perhaps a little less than it is now. But we have made some advances in the way of making gas since then.
Q. (By MR. MORSE.) What was the degree of illuminating power of that gas?
A. That was about sixteen or seventeen candle gas.
Q. What did you include, as the elements of the cost?
A. Well, sir, I included the material, labor, office expenses, and repairs.
Q. Any thing else?
A. Well, all the expenses incidental, except interest on capital.
Q. You did not include interest on capital?
A. Oh, no, sir; never do in making up the cost of the gas.
Q. Then when you speak of the cost of the gas as $1.50 per thousand feet, you do not include interest on capital.
A. Certainly not. I mean, interest on the capital of the stock of the company.
Q. Does your dollar and a half include an allowance for loss by leakage?
A. Yes, sir.
Q. How much do you allow for that?
A. Well, sir, we generally allow the actual loss.
Q. No; I ask how much you allow in this estimate of $1.50 per thousand feet?
A. The usual estimate for loss is about 10 per cent.
Q. Do you mean that you allow fifteen cents for that loss?
A. No, sir, of course not; you know I don't.

Q. How much do you allow of the $1.50 for loss by leakage?

A. We estimate the actual cost of the gas we lose.

Q. Perhaps I do not make myself clear. You have stated that you estimate the cost of gas at $1.50 per thousand feet; in making up that cost, you have allowed for various items, one of which is loss by leakage?

A. Yes, sir?

Q. Can you state what portion of the $1.50 you allow for leakage'?

A. I will tell you an estimate I made. I took the loss for one year in New York, and it was just four and a half per cent; but that is remarkably low. I think I could lay another set of pipes that would be just as well as that, sir.

Q. That hardly answers the question : Out of the $1.50, how much is allowed by you for leakage in the estimate which you made?

A. Well, sir, ten per cent.

Q. Do you mean by that, fifteen cents on the $1.50.

A. That would be one tenth, of course.

Q. Now, how much do you allow for the cost of the coal?

A. Well, sir, we take from ten to eleven thousand feet from the ton.

Q. Is not that a large estimate?

A. No, sir.

Q. Is not a fair estimate about eight thousand five hundred feet?

A. No, sir; I can show you where I have produced over ten thousand five hundred feet to the ton from the beginning of one year to the end.

Q. How much do you allow for the cost of the coal per thousand feet of gas?

A. Well, one tenth of seven and three-fourths.

Q. Do you mean seventy-five cents for the cost of the coal?

A. What it would be if the coal cost $7.75 per ton and you get ten thousand feet to the ton.

Q. How much would that be a thousand feet?
A. That is the statement.
Q. You allow for the production of ten or eleven thousand feet of gas from one ton of coal?
A. Yes, sir.
Q. What degree of illuminating power of gas?

MR. COLLINS. The witness has got about tired of being led away in this fashion. He is a practical man, and has got about disgusted with answering questions of this sort.

ALD. PETERS. I think the examination has been leading on to very interesting results. Mr. Kennedy may have thought that the manner of the counsel was such as to be a little harsh; but I am certain that the gentleman, with whom I am very well acquainted, did not mean any such thing as that. The line of questions which he is pursuing is certainly leading directly to the information that we want; perhaps Mr. Kennedy will go on and give us the entire price of the gas.

MR. MORSE. I would suggest to my learned friend that if he will allow the Aldermen to stop me, I am perfectly ready to stop when I put any question which they think is improper. But I submit that the question is a proper one, and this interruption of a witness seems to me extraordinary. In my zeal in putting questions, my manner may have been unpleasant, but it was not intended. I don't desire to put any questions except what are in the proper line of inquiry. Mr. Kennedy has no reason to assume that there is any different feeling on my part. I should judge, now, that the trouble with Mr. Kennedy was to give further information, rather than disgust with the proceedings.

MR. COLLINS. Mr. Kennedy is going to make some figures.

MR. MORSE. I supposed his figures were already made.

MR. COLLINS. He wants to make some more.

Mr. Collins stated the candle-power of gas manufactured by the several New York companies as follows: New York

Gas Light Co., sixteen-candle power; Manhattan, sixteen and four-tenths; Metropolitan, seventeen; Harlem, seventeen; New York Mutual, nineteen and five-tenths.

Mr. Collins also read communications from the clerk of the department of lamps in New York, and the proprietors of several of the hotels, theatres, and public buildings, giving their testimony as to the quality and economy of the gas manufactured by the New York Mutual Co.

MR. MORSE. I do not understand that you propose to make gas here that is like the gas made by the New York Mutual Co.

MR. COLLINS. We propose to make gas just as good, give us a chance. We propose to avail ourselves of all the modern means and appliances and improvements for making gas; and if it is found that, with the aid of naphtha, better gas can be made, naphtha will be used; if it is found that something that has not yet been discovered, that is going to be discovered, will help make gas of better illuminating power at less cost, that will be used. In other words, the best and cheapest gas that can be made will be furnished to the consumers. The object of introducing this evidence is to show that the New York Mutual Co. is supplying a gas of 19.5 candle power, which is 2.5 candle power more than any other company is supplying, at a cost from twenty to twenty-five per cent less than either of the old companies with which it is in competition. It has been shown by the testimony of Mr. Kennedy here, that that company has been making money, and adding to their facilities to supply gas to other people. Now, that is exactly what we prove; that they have given the best gas to the consumers of any of the New York companies; that they are supplying gas of a higher illuminating power at a less price; and what they have done there we are capable of doing here.

I will make this statement in behalf of the company. The company propose, as we say, to immediately invest one million dollars, and go as far as one million dollars will take them; then to go to the Legislature, and get their capital stock increased to two or two and a half millions, then go as far as the two million or two and a half millions will take them. They propose to lay a hundred miles of pipe at once; and, as they get custom, they will increase their facilities for accommodating other parts of the city. Their object is to enter into successful and vigorous competition with the Boston Gas Light Co. There is money enough to put them into that competition; and they are willing to put up any forfeiture that the city of Boston, by its Board of Aldermen may indicate as a guaranty of their good faith.

Q. Now, will you please state in regard to the allowance for coal?

A. I have made some figures hastily here which I will read. I estimate, sir, and will guarantee, to make ten thousand feet to the ton of coal; that would be at $7.50 per ton, 75 cents per thousand feet for the coal. I estimate 25 cents per thousand for labor, 20 cents for distribution, 15 cents for leakage, which I think is high, about 18 cents for taxes per thousand feet; and then I add about 20 cents for Cannel Coal. That makes $1.73. Then for coke and tar I estimate from 20 to 23 cents back.

Q. (By Mr. Morse.) Do you allow any thing for lime?

A. No, sir, I use a better article.

Q. Well, do you allow any thing for that?

A. No sir, it don't cost us any thing.

Q. What is the article?

A. It is an oxide and a sulphate of iron that we use.

Q. Does that have to be prepared?

A. It does, sir, but it goes into construction account, and I have never known it to give out yet. I use it over and over again. It is something of my own arrangement. I do not estimate that our purification costs us any thing, and it has the merit of being no nuisance. As soon as the cover is lifted, you can go and eat your dinner by the purifier, and there is no smell to it. It don't make a nuisance in the neighborhood, as is ordinarily the case with lime purification.

Q. Do you allow any thing for interest on capital?

A. I do not, because we do not generally do that in making up our estimate of cost. That is a matter of dividends; that comes afterwards. We make no account of interest, unless we borrow money.

Q. Do you allow any thing for repairs?

A. Well, sir, I think we have margin enough there for repairs. They don't amount to much.

Q. How much Cannel Coal do you allow for?

A. About a ton.

Q. I know; but what percentage of Cannel Coal is that?

A. Well, sir, it depends upon the coal we use. Five per cent would be sufficient of some Cannel Coal, and I know of one kind of which two per cent would be enough.

Q. What price coal do you allow for?

A. Well, sir, Cannel Coal runs all the way from $14 to $20 a ton.

Q. What do you allow for in your estimate, — how high priced coal?

A. Well, that is a matter of experience. I cannot —

Q. What I want to get at is the basis of your figuring. You say you allow twenty cents for Cannel Coal?

A. Yes, sir, per thousand.

Q. I want to know what proportion of Cannel Coal you allow for in your estimate?

A. Well, if it was $20 a ton for Cannel Coal, that would be ten per cent, wouldn't it?

Q. Certainly it would; so I want to know whether you do allow for $20 dollars a ton?

A. Well, if it was $10 a ton for Cannel, you would have to use just double the quantity, because the price is scaled just according to the quality of the coal; that would be

20 per cent of ten-dollar Cannel. I will stake my professional reputation, and my money too, that I will carry out these figures.

Q. What do you mean by an allowance of 20 per cent for distribution; what do you include under that head?

A. That is office expenses: taking the meters and keeping the accounts.

Q. You don't include any thing in the way of construction in this estimate, — the expense of laying mains or laying pipes?

A. No, sir; that comes into the construction account. You asked me the price of making gas. Now what have pipes to do with making gas?

MR. MORSE. I only wanted to know your elements.

Q. (By MR. PUTNAM.) Is this estimate of yours for the same quality of gas your company is furnishing in New York?

A. I stated to the gentleman that, when we had a fair share of the business, the company could manufacture gas for $1.50 per thousand; that was my statement.

Q. Yes, sir. Now I ask if this estimate which you have made was based upon the idea that you were to furnish as good gas as the Mutual Company of New York furnishes?

A. Well, sir, you are aware that coal gas and naphtha gas are not the same. When you speak about quality, I do not understand you. How do you mean, sir, the same illuminating power?

Q. The same illuminating power?

A. Well, I think it would be very similar; I can't say about the candle power to one candle.

Q. If it were made with naphtha, would it cost more or less, of the same quality?

A. Well, sir, I think I could do it for less; indeed, I know I could. I could do it for less for the company, and supply the consumers for less money; their bills would be very much less, sir. The statement that Mr. Collins has read is a fair statement. The gas supplied by the Mutual Gas Co. is from twenty to twenty-five per cent less on the bills, not per thousand, but on the bills, from twenty to twenty-five per cent less than people have paid when supplied by the other companies.

Q. You say you use no Cannel Coal there, but use naphtha?

A. No, sir, we do not; we use the best American coal we can get.

Q. Then of course you must make that for less than $1.50 a thousand?

A. We do, sir.

Q. And sell it for $2.75?

A. Yes, sir.

Q. (By Mr. COLLINS.) I want to ask you this question: do you find any danger in the use of naphtha?

A. Not the slightest, sir.

Q. (By Mr. FIELD.) The actual cost of gas is less in densely settled neighborhoods than it is in sparsely settled neighborhoods, is it not?

A. Certainly, sir.

Q. The cost of laying mains where there are few takers would be much greater in proportion than where there are a good many takers?

A. Yes, sir, that is certainly so.

Q. So you can supply a dense part of the city cheaper, comparatively, than you can a more sparsely settled part of the city?

A. That is patent to every one.

Q. If you were constructing works to-day, would you try to select the dense parts of the city, and leave the outskirts to take care of themselves?

A. I don't exactly say "yes" to that, sir. I certainly would not go to the sparsely settled parts first; no man would do that; it don't require experts to convince anybody of that.

Q. Take the Roxbury Company; they supply one part

of Roxbury which is densely populated; you could make something by supplying that part of the city; but if you ran your pipes out to West Roxbury, you could not make any money out of that portion of the city.

A. Incidentally, we might, but I don't think it would pay to build works to run pipes to the sparsely settled parts of the city.

Q. Then you would confine yourself to the densely populated part of the city?

A. I don't say that we would confine ourselves to any part. We should take the best part first, and go to the other parts as we had opportunity.

Q. If the other companies were obliged to supply the outskirts, the cost to the consumer would be greater, would it not?

A. I don't know why that should follow.

Q. If you have a ledgy soil, and are compelled to blast your ditches, is not the actual cost to the consumer greater than where you lay your pipes in sandy soil?

A. Oh, if it was rocky soil, certainly. I have laid pipes where I had to blast through the entire town.

Q. The actual cost to the consumer is greater than where the pipes are laid in sandy soil?

A. Certainly, sir.

Q. Because the whole cost of digging the drains, and laying the pipes, must enter into the cost to the consumer?

A. Why, as a matter of course.

Q. I do not know as I quite understand what you mean by eighteen cents for taxes; you mean on the plant; the proportion to the thousand feet of gas?

A. Yes, sir; that is approximate.

Q. That would depend a good deal upon the cost of the plant?

A. Yes, sir.

Q. I suppose that one well-managed company can supply a city cheaper than two?

A. Well, sir, they could if they would.

Q. The office expenses and the relative cost of the construction account would be less for one company for the whole city, than for two companies for the whole city?

A. Why, as a matter of course, it would; but that is a matter that concerns the companies altogether, not the consumers.

Q. If they act reasonably, and conduct their business well, one company can take care of a territory cheaper than two?

A. I can only answer that as I did before, they could if they would.

MR. COLLINS. I will read the names at the heads of the petitions presented at the State House last winter in aid of the petition of the Citizens' Gas Light Company, and close the case for the petitioners. Those petitions were signed by some 3,000 people. I will state that somebody has stolen the petitions. We have had the Senate door-keeper, and the custodian of the papers at the State House, hunting for these petitions, and they cannot find them; somebody has stolen them. It was not the Citizens' Gas Light Company.

MR. PUTNAM. I suppose, by the emphasis you lay on the Citizens' Gas Light Company, that you mean to imply that they were stolen by some gas company.

MR. COLLINS. From our experience of the South Boston Gas Light Company, our people over there would be most likely to suppose so.

MR. PUTNAM. You mean to insinuate that we stole those petitions?

MR. COLLINS. Yes, I shouldn't wonder if it was the South Boston Gas Light Company that stole those petitions; I do not think that the Boston Gas Light Company would do it.

ALDERMAN POWER presented several petitions in aid of the Citizens' Gas Light Company's petition, and said: I forgot to state that the gentleman who gave me those petitions requested me to state that the signatures had all been obtained within the last six hours.

ALDERMAN STEBBINS also presented petitions in aid of the petition of the Citizens' Gas Light Company.

MR. MORSE. Before the petitioners close, I would like to call their attention to a statement made the other evening, in regard to the subscriptions. We are quite content to leave the matter, so far as we are concerned, with the testimony as they have put it in; but I desire to call the attention of the Aldermen to the fact that, according to the stenographic report of the last meeting, the question was put to Mr. Carpenter, " What do you mean by your charter providing for a million of dollars ? "

[The report is read as follows:]

"*A*. I mean to say, the by-laws of our company. I mean to say, that a million of dollars would not begin to give us the amount of money we desire.

" *Q*. Have you already subscriptions to the amount of a million of dollars?

" *A*. We have, sir.

" *Q*. Where is that paper?

" *A*. It is where we can produce it at the proper time.

" *Q*. Have you any objection to producing it?

"*A*. Yes, sir, I have. I don't think it is proper to produce a private document for the opposite side to read. I am very willing to show it to a committee of the Board of Aldermen at the proper time.

" *Q*. I was going to ask, if you had any objection to the Board of Aldermen seeing it?

" *A*. Not in the least. It must come before them at the proper time, I suppose."

I have no private curiosity whatever to be gratified upon this point; but, before this hearing closes, we shall submit to the board, that the question whether or not there are *bona fide* subscriptions, as stated here, to the amount of a million dollars, is a question of some importance in determining what shall be done upon this subject; and, while I say that I do not desire from any private motives to see any document which they consider that they can properly keep from me, it seems to me eminently proper that the Board of Aldermen should see this paper, and that I should call the attention of the counsel for the petitioners to this statement, and inquire whether that paper will be presented.

Mr. COLLINS. I am glad to find the solicitor for the Boston Gas Light Company so solicitous for the information of the Board of Aldermen. The subscription list of the Citizens' Gas Light Company is in the hands of Mr. George O. Carpenter. It may be seen by yourself, Mr. Chairman, or by your eleven associates, at any time. It shall not be seen by Mr. Morse, nor the company he represents; nor by Mr. Putnam, or the company he represents. We regard it as, so far, a private paper belonging to the Citizens' Gas Light Company; that it is not proper that it should be shown to the counsel, or to the directors of any rival company. In other words, we do not propose to tell our private affairs to our enemies. We do not regard the Aldermen as our enemies; we regard them as a Board to pass upon this question; and we are perfectly willing to give that subscription list, and every guaranty we have that the money will be raised, at any time they please, to the Aldermen, or to his Honor, the Mayor; but it is not to be produced for the information of the Boston Gas Light Company, or any other organization. When the Aldermen say it is the proper time, we will produce the document.

MR. MORSE. Then I trust that the Aldermen will ask that it may be produced now; and they will take proper care that no improper person shall be allowed to see it. I do not care to see it, if there is any reason why I should not; but I trust the Aldermen will ask the petitioners to show it to them, or that it may be placed in the hands of the Chairman, to be shown to the Board at the proper time.

MR. COLLINS. When the Aldermen call for it, they can have it.

ALDERMAN POWER. I think the statement of the gentleman [Mr. Collins] will be satisfactory to the Board. To save time, I would make the motion, that that paper be deposited with the Chairman, in confidence, to be submitted to this Board at the proper time. I think that would be satisfactory to the Board; it would be to me. I should rather prefer, to save time, that it should not be submitted here. Of course the Board look upon this matter as one of as great importance as the counsel for the Boston Gas Light Company does; and I do not suppose they will decide it hastily, or until they get all the facts and information that it is possible to get on this subject, and until they are entirely satisfied that it is a *bona fide* thing.

THE CHAIRMAN. Does the Alderman withdraw his motion?

MR. COLLINS. I will say, Mr. Chairman, that, without a motion, I will hand the subscription list to you, to be shown in confidence to your associates, at any time.

MR. MORSE. I do not understand that the Aldermen bind themselves, upon that statement, that they will not speak of it. I submit, for the consideration of the Aldermen, that it is a very peculiar state of things if petitioners can come up before the Board and propose to submit their case in secret, in confidence, and the Aldermen are to be precluded from speaking about it. Suppose the Aldermen doubt the genuineness of some of the subscriptions, and desire to investigate them, does the qualification which the counsel proposes to put upon his submission, preclude them from making any inquiry, or, if any remark is made outside, are they to be charged with having divulged some secret? While I say again, that I disclaim any desire to interfere with any of the private affairs of the company, I submit that it is not right or just that the counsel should submit a paper to the Board of Aldermen in confidence, with the understanding that they are not to be allowed to speak of it.

MR. COLLINS. As a citizen of Boston, I believe that the Board of Aldermen are competent to take care of themselves. They are not under the care of the counsel for the Boston Gas Light Company. I propose to put this paper in the hands of the Chairman, to be shown to his associates. I propose to trust to his honor. I am willing to trust the Board of Aldermen that they will examine this paper for their own information; and I propose, without any other qualification than that, to submit it to the Board of Aldermen.

Mr. PUTNAM. And they are to exercise their judgment as to what use they will make of it?

Mr. COLLINS. Certainly; I believe they are gentlemen. I have confidence enough in them to believe that they will not give our secrets to your company.

REMARKS OF MR. NATHANIEL C. NASH.

Mr. Chairman. From the number of petitions that have been presented here this evening, and from the petitions that went to the Legislature last winter, it is evident to the Board of Aldermen, and to every gentleman here present, that there is dissatisfaction in this community in regard to the supply of gas to the consumers, and hence you see very responsible names signed to the petitions in behalf of this new applicant for the city's indulgence within its borders. If I were to take a position in the City Hall to-morrow, and canvass outside with petitions, asking the city to build gas-works to supply its citizens, I do not question that I could come here with ninety per cent of the consumers of gas in favor of that petition; and for the reason that it was the city that was to supply the gas, and that, too, at a minimum cost, as it does water, and to disarm all future efforts, of any kind, to get within the city for the purpose of planting a second or a third gas company within its borders.

Mr. Chairman, the question before this Board of Aldermen, and this community involves, first, the consideration of a question of political economy; and, secondly, a sanitary consideration. On the question of economy, if you were to permit a second gas company to lay its pipes in the streets, it would not cost the city less than two million dollars in the damage to the paving caused by digging up the streets; for every Alderman knows, that when you once break the ridge of a paved street, it is a broken street ever after, unless it is relaid. Now, if you have two gas companies, or two water-pipes, to supply the city, the streets in this very narrow-streeted city would be up three-fourths of the time, for one or the other of the companies. It would be consummate nonsense, and a vast damage to the city besides. Now, it is well known, certainly to most gentlemen here, that I early took an interest in this matter of the supply of gas to the city. In fact, I believe I was the first person in the United States that ever agitated the question of legislation in regard to the regulation of gas companies, when I was in the Legislature of 1856. Since that time the agitation has been started in other cities, as the result of the views that have been presented at the hearings heretofore had in this building; and now it has become a universal question throughout the United States, how to procure cheaper gas, gas of a better quality, and the means of controlling it by the citizens who are supplied with this great necessary and luxury, as it is.

The gas of a well-lighted city like ours is the best police you can have. It is watch and ward over you every night, the best watch and ward you can possibly have within your borders. Then it should be increased in quantity; it should be increased to a great extent, in order to retain that protection; and, when the city itself is the supplier of that article, and it is furnished at cost, then you can multiply your lights in the streets four-fold what they are now, and your streets will be better guarded than they are to-night.

Then, when you come to look at this question in a sanitary point of view, there are something like thirty-six gas companies that are emptying their washings into the Harbor of Boston every day in the year, and every moment of time. I undertake to say that the waters of this harbor are poisoned from Long Wharf to the outer light, from the washings of these gas companies. It is within the knowledge of the gentlemen of the Board, that after you introduced the free baths of the city, numbers of people were poisoned by taking into their mouths the poisonous stuff that floats upon the surface of the water. This fact was published in our newspapers, and it was commented upon very generally. I do not mean, of course, that these thirty-six gas companies are located in the city of Boston, but in the city of Boston and the surrounding cities and towns; all their streams empty into Boston Harbor; and the discharge of all these impurities into the water of the harbor has its effect upon the health of the city of Boston. Then I undertake to say that, when you lay gas pipes in a street, they are a nuisance, they are a positive poison to that street. Gas is an article that will escape from any iron pipe that has ever been laid down in any street, apart from what are commonly denominated leaks; and consequently the pipes should be laid in the centre of the street, so that no poison from the gas can penetrate to the buildings. It is an article that is so poisonous to water, that there is not an hour in the whole year that there are not lawsuits pending in the city of London between the gas companies and the water companies, in consequence of the gas companies poisoning the water of that city. This has been demonstrated over and over again, hundreds of times, in the water of the city of London. Will you allow a second gas company to lay down pipes in the narrow streets of this city, and thus subject your water, which is such a luxury, to the danger of poison by means of the gas? You cannot lay a second gas pipe within the city of Boston without passing over existing pipes. The pipes that a new gas company would lay would be close to the other gas pipes, and the water pipes would be brought into close contact with them in many places. This is a serious objection.

Then, again, when you come to consider that you have got to support two companies instead of one, when, if they serve the city as they should (although it is not the practice of corporations to serve the public, but to serve themselves), one company must supply the city cheaper than two can, — that is certain, — you find another serious objection.

Now, our gas companies are manufacturers and distillers of gas; and they are a class of companies that are more complained of, probably, than any other in the United States; and I do not wonder that they are complained of, for the public have been imposed upon by them more than by any other corporations that have undertaken to supply the citizens with any great necessity. They do not embrace, they will not embrace, any modern improvement in regard to the manufacture of gas, if it militates at all against their corporate interests. Now, I will read in support of my position, from a high authority in political economy, in reference to this subject of cities supplying citizens with gas.

" When, in any employment, the regime of independent small producers has either never been possible, or has been suspended, and the system of many work-people under one management has become fully established, from that time any further enlargement in the scale of production is generally an unqualified benefit. It is obvious, for example, how great an economy of labor would be obtained if London were supplied by a single gas or water company, instead of the existing plurality. While there are even as many as two, this implies double establishments of all sorts, when one only, with a small increase, could probably perform the whole operation equally well; double sets of machinery and works, when the whole of the gas or water required could generally be produced by one set only; even double sets of pipes, if the companies did not prevent this needless expense, by agreeing upon a division of the territory. Were there only one establishment, it could make lower charges consistently with obtaining the rate of profit now realized. But would it do so? Even if it did not, the community in the aggregate would still be a gainer, since the shareholders are a part of the community, and they would obtain higher profits, while the consumers paid only the same. It is, however, an error, to suppose that the prices are even permanently kept down by the competition of these companies. Where competitors are so few, they always end by agreeing not to compete. They may run a race of cheapness to ruin a new candidate, but as soon as he has established his footing, they come to terms with him. When, therefore, a business of real public importance can only be carried on advantageously upon so large a scale as to render the liberty of competition almost illusory, it is an unthrifty dispensation of the public resources that several costly sets of arrangements should be kept up for the purpose of rendering to the community this one service. It is much better to treat it at once as a public function ; and if it be not such as the government itself could beneficially undertake, it should be made over entire to the company or association, which will perform it on the best terms for the public. In the case of railways, for example, no one can desire to see the enormous waste of capital and land (not to speak of increased nuisance) involved in the construction of a second railway to connect the same places already united by an existing one; while the two would not do the work better than it could be done by one, and, after a short time, would probably be amalgamated. Only one such line ought to be permitted; but the control over that line never ought to be parted with by the State, unless on a temporary concession, as in France; and the vested right which Parliament has allowed to be acquired by the existing companies, like all other proprietary rights which are opposed to public utility, is morally valid only as a claim to compensation."

I might rest this whole argument upon this paragraph, which I have read from John Stuart Mill, because he has put it before this Board of Aldermen in such a concise manner that it settles the question to my mind, and I feel it does to yours, that the city should not permit the expenditure of such an amount of money in our streets, but that the matter of the supply of gas should be taken by the city, as they have taken the supply of water, into their own hands, and dispense it to the citizens as they do water. Go back, gentlemen, to the beginning of the war. Suppose that the supply of Boston with water had been in the hands of a corporation, what do you suppose you would have had to pay for water to-day? More than double what you are paying now; because, when you have piped your warehouses, your State House, and every public building in the city of Boston, and a corporation finds that it is supplying you with water, and you have abandoned all your wells, they are masters of the situation, and can charge what they please. Then, if the public become dissatisfied with the result, it has to obtain a second water company. Would it be of any benefit to the city of Boston to have a second water company here? Certainly not; it would be a great disadvantage. Would it be a benefit to us to have a second gas company here? Certainly not; it would be a great disadvantage.

Now, Mr. Chairman, while I am here talking about this matter of gas, I understand something of what this new company means. Here are three burners. I go into the works where they are finished, in the city of Boston, and that burner should be marked "coal gas," that should be marked "petroleum oil," and that should be marked "air;" thirty-three and a third per cent of each of them. Now, when they come to sell you gas, they burn here in this hole the air that passes over the meter. Now what goes into this hole passes over the meter, and measures just as much as the gas does; and you pay for the foot of air which costs them nothing. Tell me that they cannot make this gas for less than $1.50 a thousand cubic feet! I know better; and I will give you the proof, Mr. Chairman. Our firm this fall put into our sugar-house at East Cambridge, gas works for the supply of our sugar refinery. The works have cost us about $6,700. We were paying the Cambridge Gas Light Company about $6,000 a year for the gas we consumed within that building. We calculate that we shall save the whole cost of putting in these new works — $6,700 — the first eighteen months of their running. We have had these works running but a short time, and I meant before I appeared before the Board of Aldermen, to have had the illuminating power of this gas tested; but not having a photometer within the building, I could not do it; and I have not arrived at that fact, nor have I arrived at the actual cost.

Mr. COLLINS. How much did you pay?

Mr. NASH. We paid the city charges; we had no deductions. But, Mr. Chairman, in November, 1873, we consumed in thirty days, 186,600 cubic feet of gas of the Cambridge Gas-works supply, averaging 6,220 feet a day. From November 1, 1874, to November 13, 1874, we have consumed 25,500 feet of gas.

I will begin with the first day of November. We consumed on the first day of November, 1,500 cubic feet; on the second, 2,100 ft.; on the third, 2,100 ft.; on the fourth, 2,100 ft.; on the fifth, 2,100 ft.; on the sixth, 2,100 ft.; Saturday and Sunday, November seventh and eighth, 2,900 ft.; on the ninth, a dark day, 2,300 ft.; on the tenth, 2,100 ft.; on the eleventh, 2,000 ft.; on the twelfth, 2,200 ft.; on the thirteenth, 2,000 ft.

Gentlemen will see that our consumption ran very evenly from November 1, until November 13; to carry it through the month,— and the thirteenth brings us along nearly one-half of it,— we shall have consumed about 55,000 cubic feet of gas against 186,000 for which we paid the Cambridge Gas Light Co. in November, 1873. You see what an immense saving there is in this gas. I do not think this gas will cost us to exceed 55 cents per 1000 cubic feet, but I will call it 75 cents. When such a saving as this can be made, it is certainly clear that it is desirable that the city of Boston should undertake to supply the citizens with gas. It is a little too expensive to pay for gas in the modern way of manufacture. I venture to say if the city of Boston would supply gas at the minimum cost, it would be a saving of a million and a half of dollars every year, after they had got their works under way. I do not to mean to say that there would be a saving of a million and a half in the cost of the gas consumed for illuminating purposes, but I do undertake to say, that, when you can have gas for $1.50 or $2 a thousand feet, there is not a man in Boston, rich or poor, who can afford to buy a stick of wood or a pound of coal, because gas is the best and cheapest heat he can have in his dwelling, either for heating, or for the purpose of cooking his food. It can be done, and it should be done, in every city that provides economically for the welfare of its community. It is one of the greatest luxuries and blessings that we have. It makes us more democratic, for during the long winter evenings, at lectures and places of amusement, all classes are brought together. It is an article that should be furnished by every city in the United States at the lowest possible cost to its citizens, and not be left within the control of grasping corporations, who have too long taxed the people for this necessary article. I hope and trust that by these investigations that have been going on and are still progressing in regard to this matter, the city of Boston will be induced to take this thing in hand; and, if they will do it, I will guarantee to them the saving of one extensive park for the citizens of Boston every year; and they may go on for a hundred years, and add a new one every year that they supply the city with gas. I am sure of it.

Now, I think I have made an exhibit here in regard to what our gas costs us, and let me tell you that we are making that gas from petroleum oil, and nothing else. We are making a fixed gas, as much a fixed gas as Mr. Greenough is making to-day from any coal, and of as good quality. There is no danger from the gas; there is no condensation to that gas; and it is an illuminating gas of a power that gratifies the eye of the consumer; and, when I tell you that the gas used in our factory has proved abundantly satisfactory, I think it is proof enough to you. These gas companies know these facts; they know the facts in regard to the modern improvements in the manufacture of gas. They know that by the introduction of petroleum oil into their retorts, they can manufacture gas more cheaply than by the use of coal; and, these facts being known, people are anxious to go into the manufacture of this article to supply the city of Boston, the most profitable city in the United States to light. That is the reason why they knocked so loudly at the door of the State House last winter; that is the reason they are knocking here to-day; and no small amount of money was spent upon the Senate of Massachusetts last winter in order to carry the bill through the Senate. They have come here before you in order that they may get your consent, so that they can go to the Legislature and say, "We have got the authority of the city of Boston to build gas-works within the city; now give us the charter we asked for last winter." I opposed them before the committee last winter, as I oppose them here. It was said that I was a stockholder in the Boston Gas Light Company, but many of you know how I became a stockholder in that company. I bought a share in that stock, when I was fighting that company, on this very idea that I might have a chance to get at their books if I wanted to, when I could not do it unless I was a stockholder; and, if they refused it, I could go to the courts, and obtain my rights. I knew that, and that is what made me a shareholder in the Boston Gas Light Company. That is the sum and substance of it; it was made a handle of at the State House last winter, but I soon conquered it.

I will not detain you any longer. I have presented to you these facts in regard to my own manufacture for my own purposes and my own benefit. I say that it is patent to every one that the city of Boston could do the same. We are spending a vast deal of money, the city is vastly in debt; but when you go to work and spend money for the construction of gas works, every dollar of it will be returned to you in five years. The chairman of the committee at the State House told me last winter, "Mr. Nash, if the city of Boston was here with its petition that it might supply the city with gas at the minimum cost, we would thrust the Citizens' Company back, and give the city a charter, or the privilege, whatever it might be;" and so they would, of course.

I have nothing further to add in regard to this matter; and I close, Mr. Chairman, here.

OPENING ARGUMENT OF R. M. MORSE, Jun., Esq., FOR THE REMONSTRANTS.

I shall occupy the attention of the Board but a very few minutes before calling some witnesses. Of course, it is unnecessary for me to say that the gentleman who has just addressed the Board comes here, as he has a perfect right to do, to present his own views in regard to this question; and that while he joins with the remonstrants, and comes in, objecting to the granting of this permission, he does so not as a friend of the Boston Gas Light Company, but because he is opposed to any private corporation furnishing gas to the city. His argument is an unanswerable argument, we suppose, upon a part of the case; but it does not cover all the ground which we should desire to cover in our testimony. We suppose that there are three questions upon which the Board must pass before granting this petition: the first is, whether or not the petitioners have shown that they have the pecuniary ability to carry out their plans. That is something which has not yet been shown to the Board: the petitioners themselves have declined to furnish publicly the statement, but have promised to do so to the Board alone. It is not for me at this time to anticipate what that statement may be; nor can I tell if the Aldermen will or will not give us any information on that subject after they have seen the statement. Of course, it is primarily, and, in one sense, finally, for their own satisfaction alone; but we submit to the Board that it is the first and all-important consideration, that they should be satisfied that the petitioners have absolute and unqualified subscriptions to an amount sufficient, in the judgment of the Board, to enable the new organization to carry out its proposed work. It is very easy for a man to say, "We can get so and so;" or "I will take so much stock in a given emergency;" or, "if certain conditions are complied with, then I will be willing to subscribe:" but I take it that the Board of Aldermen, before granting permission to an organization to do what has never been done before, — to go anywhere within the limits of the city, and dig up the streets, — will be satisfied that there are absolute and unqualified subscriptions to the amount at least of one million dollars. Perhaps it would not be improper for me to suggest that the imagination of the gentleman has been somewhat drawn upon in order to find that subscription, when Mr. Leopold Morse, one of the most substantial of the petitioners, stated here the other night that he had never seen or heard of any such paper; and yet he is one of the corporators, one of the petitioners for this privilege, and a gentleman who, I need not say, would be as likely to be called upon for his subscription as any one among those who are on the petition. He states that no such paper, to his knowledge, is in existence. That there is a paper of some kind, I do not doubt. I do not believe any gentleman would misstate a fact to the Board. What I mean is, that, when you come to look at the paper itself, you will not find unqualified subscriptions which you or anybody can rely upon as meaning business. With that suggestion I leave that point to the Board.

The second point is this: It has been said here that it can be demonstrated that gas can be furnished to the city at a less price than the rates charged by the Boston Gas Light Company. There have been certain estimates put in by the gentleman called here from New York, which we believe to be unreliable, and which we think can be shown to be incorrect. We think the testimony will satisfy the Aldermen that the price of gas in the city of Boston has been not only very much less than it has been in other cities, but that it is as low as, under the circumstances of the case, it should be. I have a pamphlet here which was issued in Washington this present year, stating the price of gas in all the cities of the United States; and so far as I know, or have reason to believe, it is an entirely accurate statement. From that the Aldermen will ascertain that the highest price of gas in the country is in North Carolina, where the charge is ten dollars per thousand feet; and the lowest price in the country is at Pittsburg, Penn., in the midst of the coal regions, where the price is $1.60 a thousand. These are the maximum and minimum prices. The average in the United States is 4.32\frac{1}{2}$. So, then, the price in Boston is $2.50 per thousand, as against an average of 4.32\frac{1}{2}$ throughout the country.

ALDERMAN PETERS. Will the counsel state the price in Philadelphia?

Mr. Morse. I was about to give the prices in the principal cities. In Philadelphia, where the gas-works are owned by the city, and where, of course, the cost of coal is very much less than here, the cost is $2.30 per thousand feet. The price in New York has been stated by Mr. Kennedy as $2.75 per thousand, where there are several companies, and where there is competition. The price in Washington is $3.00 per thousand. The price in Baltimore, where, I suppose, the cost of coal is much less than it is in Boston, is $2.75 per thousand. If I am not mistaken, there is a competing company in Baltimore. The price in Chicago is $3.00 per thousand. The price in St. Louis is $3.09, where there are two companies. So that, if you take the prices of the large cities through the country, including among them Philadelphia, which has the greatest facilities of any large city in the country for manufacturing its gas cheaply, you will see that the price of gas in Boston is lower than it is in any one of them, with the single exception of Philadelphia; and there it is only twenty cents a thousand lower.

Mr. Collins. There are two companies in St. Louis; but the pipes are laid in different sections of the city, and they are not in competition.

Mr. Morse. Very likely that is so. I did not know that fact; but the price is $3.09 a thousand. Then, still further, upon the price, it is a fact that the Boston Gas Light Company has never paid to its stockholders, with the single exception of one year, more than ten per cent dividends. One year, I believe, it paid eleven per cent: that is the largest amount that has been paid. Whether it has or has not earned more than it has paid in dividends, it has never paid dividends to its stockholders to more than that amount.

In reference to the quality of the gas, testimony will be submitted, which, we think, will satisfy you that it is superior to that which is furnished in any of these cities; at least equal, and it is claimed superior. All these considerations will bear upon this point, — whether or not the price of gas in the city now is greater than it should be.

But, Mr. Chairman, passing from that question, there is a third one upon which we suppose the Aldermen are to pass before granting this petition, and that is, whether, in any aspect of the case, assuming for the moment that the petitioners can prove, and you should be satisfied, that the price of gas is more than it should be, even then, the petitioners' prayer should be granted. We say that, even in that case, there are reasons altogether sufficient why it should not be granted. That is to say, if you should find an evil to exist, that is not the proper remedy to apply.

This ground has been to some degree covered by the remarks that have already been made by Mr. Nash. Let me, however, remind you again, that if you have in any business sufficient capital embarked to do that business, thoroughly and properly, it is perfectly clear that, if you put in additional capital, the cost of the product must be increased to the consumer. Now, it will not be denied that there are gas-works enough, and gas-pipes enough laid in the streets, to supply the city of Boston with gas. It will not be denied that there are facilities for supplying the city which are as good as any other company can furnish. How, then, will you diminish the price of gas by doubling those facilities? If one pipe laid in a street is sufficient to furnish gas to all the consumers on that street, how will you cheapen the price of gas to those consumers by laying an additional pipe? Of course I understand the answer which is made, and which, on a superficial view, seems to be sufficient, that competition can exist here as in any kind of trade. There is a fallacy, however, in that argument. In regard to many branches of trade, there is no absolute limit in regard to the business that they can do, or the amount of consumption. Take the matter of horse-railroad companies: no horse-railroad company petitions this Board for leave to construct an additional railroad through the same streets as those occupied by an existing company, from the same terminus to the same terminus, to supply just the same customers, to carry the same passengers.

What would you do with a petition of that kind? Suppose, for instance, the Metropolitan Railroad has laid down two tracks between two points. It has the facilities, therefore, for transporting all the cars that are needed for carrying the passengers between those two points. Would you permit another railroad to lay down its tracks in those same streets, between those same points, in order to make competition? Would you think that an economical or proper arrangement? You may say, and you have said, frequently, that, as between those two termini, by roads running through different streets, accommodating other passengers, and in that way stimulating travel, it may be a good thing to have competition, and you have permitted it to be done. So, again, in regard to the matter of newspapers, which was alluded to in the opening. It is said, "One newspaper is in existence; why not say that no other one should be started?" It is not necessary, of course, to say in regard to that, that there is no absolute limit to the amount of consumption there may be, and that every newspaper started meets a different want, supplies a new class of customers, and stimulates the existing journals, so that two newspapers may do more business than one did, and may do it at less rates. But, to go back to the point, of course it is out of the question that a new company should transmit their gas through the same set of pipes as the old company; and to lay another set of pipes would involve an expenditure of at least $1,000,000. It is not pretended by the gentlemen themselves that they could do this for less than $1,000,000. It is suggested, then, that you should allow another company to sink $1,000,000 here, to do a business that can be done with the capital already invested. What would be the result? One of two or three things would follow. My friends say that they could not be bought off, and they will not be bought off. Therefore it would not be proper for me to suggest that they would ever be bought off, or that any amount of money would tempt them to sell out their stock. They probably never will sell it out; they will hold on to it.

Then what will they do? Either they must come to an arrangement with the old company, by which certain districts will be supplied by the new company, and certain districts by the old company, or else they must go through the same districts with the old company. If certain districts are allotted to them, the price of gas in those districts cannot be less than it is now. If they undertake to go into the same districts, they will naturally select the most profitable. In the first place, they will look through the most thickly-settled parts of the South End and of Roxbury, and say, "There is an opportunity to make money." The Boston Gas Light Company are supplying all parts of the city; they must go where there are only half-a-dozen consumers upon a street, and where the returns are, of course, insufficient to pay the expenses of carrying the gas there; but this company will not do any thing of that kind. They will go into the heart of the city, take the cream of the business, select certain streets where there is the most dense population, and where there is the greatest consumption, and lay down their pipes there. Assuming that, for a while, they can reduce the price of gas, — and it is quite possible that for the purpose of tempting consumers, and getting a share of the business, they may do that, — yet, if they cannot manufacture the gas (and I believe it will be shown they cannot) at any considerable reduction from what it costs the Boston Gas Light Company, they will, in the end, do what other corporations do under the same circumstances. They will come to some arrangement with the old company, by which a change will be made which will support both companies; for both companies must live. These gentlemen, however philanthropic they may feel now, are really no more philanthropic than other men. They will want a return upon their investment. It is absurd to suppose that they will go on year after year without receiving any dividends. There will come a time when these gentlemen will want to get their dividends, and then they will have to come to an arrangement with the old company; and then will come a time, as suggested by Mr. Nash, when the consumer will have to pay dividends upon two capitals instead of one, and not only have to pay upon two capitals, but to make up for the loss of dividends which the new company, and possibly the old company, have sustained. The time will come when there will be so much more additional capital upon which interest must be paid. Our suggestion is this: that it is not good policy for the city to have additional pipes put down in the streets when the present pipes are sufficient. If there is any thing wrong in the management of the present company, if there is any thing to be improved there, if there is any thing excessive in the price of the gas, that is one thing; but the remedy is not in attempting to lay down additional pipes, and sinking more capital. That is the broad consideration; I need not allude to minor ones, which, of course, will occur to you.

There are some questions of positive expense to the city of Boston in its corporate capacity, as well as to individual citizens, involved in the excavation of the streets. Think what it would be to go through the principal streets of this city (and those are the ones which our friends would propose to visit first). To excavate them, and lay down the pipes, would involve great expense. They say they will guarantee the city against that expense; but every gentleman on this Board knows that if the pavement is once taken up for purposes of this description, it is not the same pavement it was before, when it has been replaced; there is a positive and serious injury to the pavement. Who is to pay for that? Does this company propose to pay for it? Not at all; and, if they did propose to pay for it, it would be virtually to pay for repaving the streets, and there is no item in their estimates for any such expense as that. That would add largely, I think, to the estimate of two million dollars, if they were to allow for the repaving of the streets through which they lay their pipes. There is, then, a positive injury, and every citizen is to be incommoded in those streets, and all for what? As I said before, it all comes down to this, to get additional pipes to do the business which can be done through the present pipes.

Then take such a minor detail as this: You have to-day one organization that is responsible, to whom you can look in case of any leak, and whom you can charge with neglect in case any thing goes wrong. But suppose there are two companies, and there is a leak in the street pipes, which company is to make the excavation? Whose leak is it? While the two companies are disputing as to who shall do the digging, immense damage may be done to property, and perhaps to life. What means are there of determining? Those pipes run through the street side by side; whose pipe is it that leaks? And if one company digs down to find the leak, and it turns out to be in the pipes of the other company, then the first company will shovel the earth back, fill up the hole, and the other company must go to work and dig it out again. The annoyance and trouble that would follow from having two organizations undertake to do the same work in the same place are infinite in number.

Again: I believe it is the experience of men conversant with streets, that there are certain planes in the streets that should be occupied for one purpose. For instance, the water pipes should be at a certain level, the gas pipes should be at a certain level, and the sewer pipes at a certain level. There are certain planes in the streets that ought to be allowed to these particular pipes. If this proposed company should lay their pipes in the streets, they may lay them either above or below the existing level. They cannot very well go above, because I suppose the present pipes are as near the surface as safety will admit. Therefore, they will have to go below, and they must disturb more or less the sets of pipes that now exist in the streets. Mr. Nash has pointed out the injury that would be done to the water pipes, but all the pipes would be affected by it. The effect of the excavation would be, at least, to disturb all these other pipes, and then after a frost, there would be trouble from breakage, and leakage, and various causes.

The point, then, Mr. Chairman, is substantially this: that even after the Board have settled upon the first two questions, as to the character and responsibility of the petitioners, and as to whether or not the citizens are well and fairly served by the present companies, the proper, adequate, or reasonable remedy for any evils that may exist is not the one proposed by these petitioners. They come here and ask your permission to do an act which would not be profitable to the citizens of Boston, or to the city itself in its corporate capacity.

Of course, Mr. Chairman, it is said, and truly said, that the companies, in appearing here to remonstrate, have a selfish interest of their own. That is all true; and at the same time it is due to the companies to say this, that they have administered their affairs in such a way, that although there have been, from time to time, complaints and investigations, yet never during the whole period of their existence has any tribunal, whether legislative or municipal, undertaken in any way to dispense with their services, or to change materially their powers.

The result of all the investigations which have been conducted by your predecessors here for years and years has been this: that while it is perfectly natural to make complaints, and to believe that the citizens can be better and more cheaply supplied, yet on the whole, taking things as they go, looking at the results in other cities, at the experience of practical men, the city of Boston is served fairly and honestly. We believe that that will be the verdict here; and, if that is so, then we say, that while this is a matter of selfish interest to the companies who appear here and remonstrate, yet it is only due to servants of the city, who have done their duty, that they shall be told there is no occasion for superseding them, or for introducing an agent or servant who would not do the work for the city for any thing less in the way of cost than it is now done.

These, gentlemen, are, in general, the grounds of this opposition, so far as the Boston Gas Light Company are concerned. There are some gentlemen present who may not take so much time as one or two of our witnesses, and I propose to call them first.

TESTIMONY OF JOHN C. PRATT.

Q. (By Mr. Morse.) You are President of the Jamaica Plain Gas Co.

A. I am.

Q. One of the companies that furnishes gas within the city limits?

A. Yes, sir.

Q. About how long has your company been organized?

A. About twenty years.

Q. What quantity of gas do you manufacture?

A. We are a small company. We are manufacturing now about 70,000 feet a day.

Q. Are you willing to state about what is the cost of the gas to you?

A. I have no objection. We went into a very careful estimate of the cost of the gas last spring, when making our bargain with the city to furnish a supply for the street-lamps, and we found that our gas cost us three dollars a thousand feet, — a trifle over that. We were asked, and urged, to furnish it to the city for two dollars and seventy-five cents a thousand feet; but we found it impossible to do it without losing money, which we were not inclined to do, — which we were afraid to do; and we told the city committee that we should decline to take two dollars and seventy-five cents per thousand feet, and so they pay us three dollars, which is about the cost.

Q. Do you manufacture the gas as economically as you can?

A. We think we do.

Q. What quality of gas do you manufacture?

A. Our gas, I think, is from sixteen to eighteen candles, — sixteen or seventeen.

Q. What is the amount of your capital stock?

A. The capital stock is $170,000. We have added about forty or fifty thousand dollars this summer, to erect an additional gas-holder.

Q. How many miles of street main have you?

A. About eighteen miles.

Q. About how much does that cost?

A. I cannot recollect the division of expense. I have not those details with me; but our capital simply represents the absolute cost of the works. We have never watered it a dollar.

Q. What is your charge to the consumer?

A. Four dollars.

Q. What dividends do you make?

A. We make four per cent every six months. That is all that we have ever made. The first years of our existence we never made anything; but we have never made over four per cent, and we have never laid up any surplus.

Q. If you were making a million of feet a day, do you think it could be made at a cost of $1.50 per thousand feet?

A. No. I have no idea that it could.

Q. Have you had any experience in New York with the Citizens' Mutual Gas Light Co.?

A. No, sir, I have not.

Q. Have you been in any of the hotels?

A. Yes, sir. I have stopped at the hotels.

Q. Have you examined into the quality of the gas?

A. I made a remark, when the certificate was read here this evening, signed by several very respectable parties representing some of the New York hotels. I was rather amused at the certificate from the Fifth Avenue Hotel; for the last time I was there I could not see with six lights, and called for kerosene lamps, which they did not have. I asked one of the proprietors what was the trouble with the gas, and he said that they had lately introduced the new gas company's gas; and he supposed that was the trouble. That is all I know about it.

CROSS-EXAMINATION.

Q. (By MR. COLLINS.) When were you at the Fifth Avenue Hotel, and found this trouble?
A. I think it was one of my last visits. I will not be positive; but certainly within a very few months. The whole incident was in my memory, and I spoke of it, smilingly, when the names of the proprietors of the Fifth Avenue Hotel were read.
Q. They told you it was probably on account of the gas that had lately been introduced there?
A. Yes, sir.
Q. Who told you that?
A. One of the proprietors.
Q. Do you know his name?
A. I do know it, but I won't tell who it was. I should not want to be brought into a personal controversy with him; but it was one of the proprietors who told me so.
Q. You say you manufacture about 70,000 feet a day
A. Yes, sir.
Q. Have you had any experience in the manufacture of gas, other than that?
A. No, sir.
Q. Are you a gas engineer?
A. No, sir.
Q. Are you familiar with the manufacture of gas?
A. Tolerably so. I built the works, or engineered them, and have been president of the company ever since they were built, and taken care of them.
Q. What are your retorts made of, iron or clay?
A. Clay.
Q. Will you be good enough to say on what ground you testify, that if you had a million feet a day instead of 70,000

feet to deliver, it could not be manufactured for $1.50 per thousand?

A. Well, that was my opinion. I have not gone into the exact figures. I have no doubt we could make it for a great deal less than we do now; but I do not think we could make it for $1.50. I was simply asked my opinion about that.

Q. Your opinion, therefore, is that of a man who has had experience as president of a company: you are not a gas engineer, and have not had any other experience?

A. I have never been connected with any company that did make a million of feet a day. I have told you that, and I have made no investigations.

Q. Therefore your opinion is just what you have stated?

A. My opinion in regard to it lies in the fact which has been stated here this evening. We have had those pamphlets read here, giving the price at which gas was manufactured and sold, and we find that the city of Boston furnishes gas cheaper than almost any city in the country. As has been stated, in the city of Philadelphia, where coal is two or three dollars a ton cheaper, and the gas is manufactured by the city and sold without any profit, they get $2.30 per thousand feet. In New York, where coal is certainly a dollar a ton cheaper, gas is twenty-five cents a thousand dearer than it is in Boston; and so right through the country.

Q. It costs you about $3.00 a thousand feet to make your gas, and you sell it for $4.00, so you make a dollar a thousand on all you deliver?

A. No, I beg you not to understand that at all. A very large portion of the gas we manufacture (I do not recollect how much, but a very large portion of it) is furnished to the city at absolute cost. We don't make a cent; we rather lose money on that.

Q. Are you a stockholder in the Boston Gas Light Co.?

A. No, sir, I never owned a dollar of the stock.

Q. Do you hold any of the stock as trustee, or in any other way?

A. No, sir, I have not the slightest interest in it. I want it to be distinctly understood, that, so far as the Citizens' Gas Light Company is concerned, if they wish to come to Jamaica Plain and furnish gas, I will hold up both hands to let them come, for the first thing I would do would be to sell them our works. When they want them, they shall have them for much less than they can build new.

Q. How much do you get out of a ton of coal?

A. We average about eight or nine thousand feet.

Q. Have you made any test, yourself, of the candle power of your gas?

A. No, I leave that to my superintendent, a very competent man.

Q. How do you know what its candle power is?

A. I simply know from what he tells me. When my superintendent comes and reports to me, I simply take his word for it.

Q. (By Mr. Putnam.) Will you tell us what coal you use?

A. We use coal from Maryland. It comes mainly from Baltimore and vicinity. In connection with that, we use a certain percentage of Cannel Coal, varying with the weather. We use more in the winter than we do in the summer.

Q. (By Mr. Field.) What do your Maryland and Pennsylvania coals cost you?

A. We calculate that our coal, delivered and stored in the sheds, costs us about $10.00 a ton; that is, for the Maryland coal. The Cannel Coal, of course, costs more.

Q. How much does the Cannel Coal cost?

A. I have forgotten what proportion we use now of Cannel Coal.

Q. (By Mr. Morse.) Can you tell us about what is the difference between the price of Maryland coal in Boston and Baltimore?

A. Well, freight now is pretty low, so our superintendent tells me, — $1.50 to $1.75; but ordinarily the freight is about $2.50, and sometimes as high as $3.00.

Q. How is it in Philadelphia?

A. The freights from Philadelphia are about the same as they are from Baltimore.

Q. (By Mr. COLLINS.) I understand you to say that freight is $1.50 from Baltimore to Boston?

A. No, I said that my superintendent told me that freights were very low just now, and that he could get a cargo for from $1.50 to $1.75, but ordinarily rates are from $2.50 to $3.00 from Baltimore.

Q. But if you are going to dig coal in Pennsylvania to be carried to Boston, you do not carry it to Baltimore first?

A. A great deal of our coal comes from the West Virginia mines, which goes to Baltimore. If we get Pennsylvania coal, it goes to Philadelphia; but the freight from Philadelphia to Boston is just about the same as from Baltimore to Boston.

Q. You know you can sell coke in Boston.

A. Not a great deal. I do not know what it brings here, but it don't bring much with us.

Q. It brings more here than in Philadelphia or Baltimore?

A. I do not know. I do not know what the price of coke is there. I know it don't bring much with us. Of course, if any great benefit was to be derived by introducing a new gas company, so that gas could be furnished cheaper, it is worthy of consideration; but when I recollect, as I do, what a perfect net-work of pipes there is in these streets, which are thirty or forty feet wide, — that we have five pipes, two gas pipes, two water-pipes, and a common sewer, with laterals running in every direction, — when, I say, I remember what a perfect net-work of pipes we have in our streets, it seems to me that, unless it could be shown, beyond all question, that some great advantages are to be derived by the citizens, from allowing an additional set of pipes to be laid down, by way of a reduction in the price of gas, the thing ought not to be thought of for a single moment. I object, as a citizen, to digging up our streets, and not as a stockholder, or as having any interest, in any way, in the Boston Gas Light Company.

Q. (By Alderman Worthington.) I would like to ask you one question. You have said that you supplied the city of Boston for $3.00 a thousand, and that a ton of coal will make nine thousand feet of gas. That is $27.00 a ton. Will you state to the Board of Aldermen how you make the difference between $9.00 and $27.00, which is the price at which, you say, you supply the city of Boston?

A. Of course, it costs more per thousand feet for a small company like ours, than a large company. I take the whole expense of our company; that is, labor, repairs, coal, lime, and every expense incident to the working of the cómpany in the manufacture of gas, and deduct from that the small sum which we receive from coke, which is a few hundred dollars a year, and then ascertain how many thousand feet of gas we make by that process, and then we arrive at the actual cost of the gas. I could furnish all these details if required, but I have not them in my mind.

Q. (By Alderman Power.) How many miles of pipe do you say your company have?

A. We have eighteen miles, over a very sparsely-settled territory — a great deal of it. Of course, as our business increases, we shall be able to manufacture gas cheaper.

Q. How many consumers do you suppose you have to a mile, compared with what they have in Boston?

A. I think we average thirty-eight consumers to the mile.

Q. (By Mr. Field.) In your cost of $3.00 per thousand feet, do you include interest on your stock?

A. No; we calculate the cost. Whatever the interest is, that is profit.

Q. That is, you exclude interest on your investment?

A. Yes, sir.

TESTIMONY OF GEORGE B. NEAL.

Q. (By Mr. Morse.) What is your connection, sir, with the Charlestown Gas Company?

A. I am treasurer, engineer, and general manager.

Q. How long have you been connected with that company?

A. Since the year 1852, — about twenty-two years.

Q. Are you practically acquainted with the processes of manufacturing gas?

A. I am.

Q. Have you devoted a good deal of attention to it?

A. Twenty-two years ago the company was organized in my office, when I was practising law. My partner was the first president, and I was treasurer. I soon left the law, and took a more congenial pursuit.

Mr. Collins. You are a lucky man.

Mr. Neal. That is what I have been told a great many times, when I have appeared as a witness, and mentioned the fact; it may be so.

Q. What is the amount of your capital?

A Five hundred thousand dollars.

Q. What is the number of your consumers?

A. Forty-one hundred, or forty-two hundred, — between four and five thousand.

Q. About how many miles do you have of street mains?

A. I think we run in Charlestown twenty miles, and in Somerville ten miles. We divide the city of Somerville with the Cambridge Company. One takes one side of the railroad, and the other the other.

Q. What is the cost of the manufacture of gas to you?

A. Well, it costs a good deal, if not more. I don't know that I ought to state the cost, as my friend Mr. Kennedy don't like to state on his side. I told him if he would give us the cost, I might.

Q. Can't you state about what it is?

A. It costs more in some places than it does in others.

Q. I will begin by asking you what is the price you charge there?

A. We charge three dollars a thousand feet to ordinary consumers, two dollars and a half to the city for street lamps, and we make a discount to large consumers.

Q. How large is the discount?

A. Five per cent.

Q. And on what amount of bills?

A. Five hundred a year. We have not a great many large consumers. We have the State Prison. The Waverley House has left us.

Q. What dividends have you paid on your stock?

A. Ten per cent. We have, I am happy to say, in former years, paid ten per cent, and now and then a little extra to keep the ten per cent in order.

Q. Have you paid on the average more than ten per cent?

A. No, we have not. I would state why we pay ten per cent. We commenced in a cautious way, and paid eight per cent; and then, for a few years, we paid some extras to make it up to ten per cent, but since the year 1865, I think, we have paid but ten per cent dividends, directly or indirectly, and I hope we never shall pay more than that. I think the policy of the company is this: to earn ten per cent, and keep the works in perfect repair, and reduce the price. Nothing would please me more than to be able to reduce the price on the first day of January to two dollars and seventy-five cents per thousand feet, or as low as the Boston Gas Light Company, because I think we shall sell more gas. We find that kerosene oil is a great rival or competitor with us. Many of our consumers burn kerosene oil as well as gas, and many people burn it altogether; and if we could only find a way to make gas at less cost, and sell it for less, I think we should gain a good deal. Therefore, I have visited the Mutual Works in New York, and a great many works, to find out some new process; and it seems to me that if petroleum can be adopted in conjunction with coal gas, or alone, it will be a benefit, although there are some drawbacks. I visited the Mutual Works on several occasions. I was there but a short time ago, and saw the process which I suppose they intend to use here. No, I don't suppose so, because they say they are not going to use it, and I believe what my brother Kennedy says. But I have also been approached by the gentleman who has the patent for making the gas from petroleum that is used in my venerable brother's works, the Sugar Refinery, that he speaks of in East Cambridge; and the gentleman owning the patent offers to take our works, and adapt them, in part, to this new process. I think all the gas companies are now striving their best to find something to make gas that is cheaper than coal; and although we charge three dollars a thousand, fifty cents more than is charged in the city of Boston proper, we are open to conviction. If there is any way by which we can compete with our brethren on this side of the water, or any new company, we shall do it, and make a crusade into Boston.

Q. Let me ask you whether any of these processes of making gas from petroleum or naphtha have been introduced into the cities of New England?

A. No; not in New England. They have been introduced into New York, Detroit, and Chicago.

Q. The Mutual Company of New York uses one of the processes, does it not?

A. They use what is called the Gale & Rand process.

Q. That is a patented process?

A. Yes, sir, a patented process. That substitutes naphtha for Cannel Coal, in part. They use coal and naphtha, and what is generally known around here as common air. The air in New York isn't quite so pure as this, therefore I don't think they make quite so good gas out of it. I think petroleum would be the best article to make illuminating gas of, if it wasn't so rich. When you carry it up to forty, fifty, sixty, or seventy candles, something must be done to bring it down, so that it can be burned in ordinary burners.

Q. You heard the opinion of Mr. Kennedy as to the price

at which gas could be made if a million feet a day were furnished, to wit, at $1.50 a thousand. I want to ask you if, in your judgment, gas could be made at that price of the quality of this gas here, out of coal?

A. I am just as certain as that I stand here that it couldn't be, and I think my brother Kennedy isn't certain of that. I don't know; he may be. The gas made by the Boston Gas Light Company is the richest gas made in New England, I know from actual test; and I have no hesitation whatever in saying, that it cannot be made for that price. The coal alone per thousand feet sold will cost very near a dollar a thousand, using Albert coal, which is very expensive. It was offered to me the other day by certain parties at $25 a ton in gold; and, using that coal, this gas cannot be manufactured for $1.50 a thousand. I am as certain of it as I am that I stand here.

Q. What amount of gas do you estimate your company make from a ton of coal?

A. I have sometimes made five feet to a pound of American coal, but unfortunately couldn't sell it all because of its loss by leaks and condensation. Five feet to the pound is a good yield where there is no enriching. I think if five feet to the pound are made constantly, it tends to reduce the quality of the gas. If we can sell four feet to the pound, of gas made from Provincial coal and from American coal, it is doing very well.

Q. If you allow two thousand two hundred and forty pounds to the ton, what percentage do you allow for Albert coal, and how much of the other?

A. I think the fault of the Boston Gas Light Company's gas is this: it is too rich; it smokes. The burners are not adapted to it. The burners in this room may do very well, but many of the burners that are used are not adapted to it. Five per cent of Albert coal is sufficient; although I have known eight per cent, and even ten, to be used. In winter there is more of that used than in summer, because the cold has a tendency to reduce the candle-power of the gas as it passes from the works into the mains to the consumers. Five per cent Albert, I should think, was a pretty strong mixture; but I have known even eight to be used. Speaking of the cost of the coal, I have no hesitation in saying, that, in making up the cost of the gas last year, we found that the cost of the coal was one dollar and some hundredths of a mill per thousand feet. I carry out my calculations to tenths of a mill, and it costs one dollar and a fraction of a mill.

Q. For the coal alone?

A. Yes, sir. Every thousand feet that any consumer in Charlestown uses costs us one dollar for coal. That I remember distinctly, because it happened to come nearly even. But I am willing to say this, that it has been said by those who are supposed to understand the business better than I do, that the coke pays for the coal; but the coke we sell for $4.00 a chaldron, delivered, and the fine is sold for $2.00 or $1.50. The coke pays us $17\frac{8}{10}$ for every thousand feet we sell. I don't care any thing about how many thousand feet we made; if we made a hundred millions, that wouldn't help us. If we made a hundred million feet, and lost all but fifty or sixty, that wouldn't help us. We made sixty millions, I think, last year, and the loss was thirteen per cent. Before the Mystic water pipes were put in, the loss used to average about eight per cent. After they put in their works the loss went up to twenty per cent; but I have succeeded in bringing it down to thirteen per cent. That shows that the coke pays for the coal — over the left.

ALDERMAN PETERS. That leaves the cost of the coal eighty-three cents?

MR. NEAL. If you don't deduct any thing for the cost of the works. Then I would say that we pay for taxes alone, fifteen cents on every thousand feet we sell. This year it will be nearer twenty, as our capital is increased. With a capital of $500,000, we pay this year, in round numbers, $10,000 in taxes to the city of Boston, the city of Somerville, and the State of Massachusetts. I think the reason why my brethren hesitate, here and elsewhere, to give the cost of gas, isn't so much that they are afraid that the public will make a bad use of it, but they don't like their brethren in the profession to know.

Q. Has the question of competing gas companies, or the policy of having two companies in the same streets, been considered in any formal way in this country?

A. It has. There have been several cases, particularly in Memphis, Tenn. I think that I was called upon to give some evidence with regard to the occupancy of streets by two rival companies. I forget what year it was, but I then wrote a letter from which I think this is an extract: —

" I have never had any experience of the kind referred to in the foregoing paper, on the subject of street mains, &c., with a *rival gas company*, but I have had some such experience with a *friendly water company.* The city of Charlestown, a few years since, introduced pure water through pipes into our streets; and, although the water-pipes were on the opposite side of the street from our gas-pipes, where it was practicable, and where our pipes were laid only on one side, yet we experienced great trouble and annoyance, both at the time and since, by reason of breakage of our mains and services, caused by settling of earth and pavements above the water-pipes, gates, hydrants, &c.; and this has occurred, although as a general rule the water-pipes have been laid much deeper than our gas-pipes. It would be impossible for me to estimate how much gas we have lost by breakage, caused as above stated. Now, as we would suffer much more every way from a rival gas company, I endorse the above statement of 'facts' to the fullest extent."

Q. What would you think of the policy of laying down other sets of gas-pipes, in the principal streets of Boston?

A. I think it would be impolitic and inexpedient. I know there was a good deal of complaint made in New York about the cost of taking up the pavement. They ran down through Fifth Avenue, and I know the pavement hadn't been laid long, and they didn't leave it in so good condition as it was before, and afterwards they or some other company, or the city raised it up to a level; but in Boston I think it would be very unwise. I am speaking of Boston proper. If this company proposes to go over to Charlestown, I think we can meet them half way, in some way that I have in view; but in Boston proper, the principal streets through which the new company proposes to run are narrow streets, and, as Mr. Kennedy observed, the streets in New York are straighter and wider. In many of the streets of Boston there are now two sets of gas-pipes, and I don't know but three. The plan for the distribution of gas in Boston is different from that which is employed in New York and many other places. In New York the gas-holders, as a general thing, are at the works, or very near them, so that the pressure may be regulated at all times; but in Boston proper, and the suburbs of Boston, there are one or two gas-holders at the works. The gas is made and delivered into the holders, and then from those holders it is delivered to all parts of the city. The Boston Gas Light Co. have a great many holders in different parts of the city, and in addition to the small pipes which run through the streets, some on one side, and some on both sides, supplying the consumers, they have large pipes, some very large, running to these holders in different parts of the city, which makes an addititional pipe in the streets.

Q. (By Mr. Putnam.) You said the number of your consumers was from four to five thousand. Can you give it nearer than that?

A. I don't always like to give figures. I will say it is nearer four thousand than five thousand.

Q. Has the number of your consumers increased largely the last three or four years?

A. The last year they haven't increased very largely. Since the panic I think they haven't increased; but previous to that, they were increasing very much in Somerville, which is out of this municipality. Somerville covers a great deal of territory, and a great deal of building has been going on there, and I think we have gained a great many consumers there.

Q. (By Mr. Collins.) They have taken to burning oil?

A. Yes, sir; and we want to find something to carry up the price of petroleum, and lower the price of gas.

Q. You say your capital stock is $500,000?

A. Yes, sir.

Q. What is the value of the property?

A. The tax commissioner estimates the value at $625,000, or rather, we are taxed for that.

Q. What do you estimate it at?

A. We estimate it at $500,000; but then there is the premium on the stock.

Q. You pay taxes on more than $600,000?

A. Yes, sir; a premium of $12.50 on a share.

Q. I don't refer to your stock. I merely refer to the value of the real and personal property held by your company.

A. It is taxed by the tax commissioners for $650,000.

Q. The personal and real property of the company is taxed at what?

A. I think it is $506,000; something like that.

Q. You say you pay about $10,000 taxes?

A. Yes, sir. Then they estimate the premium on the stock at $12.50 on a share, which would make it $125,000 additional.

Q. What, in your judgment, is your property worth?

A. We have some real estate that couldn't be bought for what we paid for it. — Yes, it could, just at this moment.

Q. Your real and personal property is worth a good deal more than $600,000, isn't it?

A. No, sir, I don't think it is. It might be. Our franchise might bring something.

Q. You paid in $500,000 in cash?

A. Yes, sir.

Q. You have been paying ten per cent dividends, and something more?

A. I said that it is about ten per cent as it stands.

Q. You say you have got twenty miles of pipe in Charlestown, and ten miles in Somerville?
A. Yes, sir.
Q. How many thousand feet a day do you average?
A. We are sending out now about 260,000 feet. We made 60,000,000, feet last year, and sold 50,000,000 odd.
Q. You said the price of Albert coal was $25.00 per ton, in gold. Is it not true that at times the whole of that coal is taken up and controlled by the Boston Gas Light Company?
A. I have been told so, but I don't know. This was a coal dealer who asked me to buy it at that high figure.
Q. Do you use this Albert coal at all?
A. No, sir. Our gas would cost $1.15 if we used Albert coal as they do in Boston.
Q. What is the price you pay for your coal?
A. We pay for American coal, as we call it, that is, Pennsylvania, and Westmoreland, that comes from Virginia, and is delivered in Philadelphia, $6.25 per ton, free on board. Then we pay freight, which varies. This year the average price has been less than $2.00.
Q. Then you get your coal delivered upon your premises for say $8.00 a ton?
A. Yes, sir. I think it averages rather more than that, because we commenced early in the season, before the price was so low.
Q. You say that at on will produce about 9,000 feet of gas; from nine to eleven?
A. Yes, 11,000 is rather high.
Q. Say 10,000?
A. Yes, sir.
Q. Now, out of a ton of coal costing on your premises $8.00, you manufacture 10,000 feet of gas, and sell it for $3.00. Do you mean to say that you can't manufacture that gas for $2.00 a thousand feet?
A. I mean to say that very freely.
Q. If, instead of selling 260,000 feet a day, you sold a million feet a day, don't you think you could manufacture the gas and sell it for $2.00 a thousand feet?

A. I think I could sell gas made from the richest Cannel Coal for $2.50, give me my choice of the streets of Boston, but not taking the outskirts. There are a good many streets that it don't pay to run gas-pipes through.

Q. Suppose you had an opportunity to come into Boston proper (you know that is fairly defined), and had guaranteed the purchase of a million feet a day, couldn't you manufacture and sell gas for $2.00 a thousand feet?

A. No, sir.

Q. You can't figure that out?

A. I can't figure that out. I have had some feeling that the Boston Gas Light Company didn't always do right, and I have been examining into that in connection with some other questions.

Q. I will ask you another question: As a practical man, if a capital of $400,000 or $500,000 will supply four or five thousand consumers in a sparsely settled district, will not a capital of four times that amount supply four times as many in a close district?

A. Yes; four times one are four.

Q. You have a capital of five hundred thousand dollars, and you have got your pipes laid in Charlestown and Somerville, haven't you?

A. In Charlestown, as I say, we have laid twenty miles of pipe, and we have laid ten miles in Somerville.

Q. Your customers are in Charlestown and Somerville. Somerville has a larger area of territory than Charlestown, hasn't it?

A. The increase in cost is greater than the increase in distance. I might state it in this way: We run one mile of pipe, and, to supply consumers on that mile, a certain size of pipe is required; but of course we can't tell the exact size, because we don't know how much the consumption will be; but if we are going to run another mile beyond the first mile, then the pipe through the first mile must be made larger; and the further we go, the larger it must be.

Q. Let me put the question, then, a little plainer. You

have five hundred thousand dollars capital, and you are supplying four or five thousand consumers in Charlestown and Somerville; could you take two millions of capital and come over to the city and build works; put your supply-pipes through the densely-populated sections of the city, and furnish gas to the persons who are now taking it from the Boston Gas Light Company, for two dollars a thousand feet?

A. No, sir; where we sell one thousand feet of gas the Boston Gas Light Company sells twelve thousand.

Q. That is, in the same mile?

A. Yes, sir.

Q. Where you sell one thousand feet they sell twelve times as much?

A. Yes, sir.

Q. I will put this question, then: You are supplying sparsely-settled sections of country on a capital of five hundred thousand dollars; if you could come into the city of Boston, with a capital of two million dollars, and build works, could you not enter into successful competition with the Boston Gas Light Company?

A. I could, by taking a particular number of streets; of course I will admit that.

Q. You make your gas out of American coal, which costs on your premises, delivered, about eight dollars a ton?

A. It does not make so good gas as the Boston Gas Light Company's product. The gas of the Boston Gas Light Company is, as I have had occasion to test, the richest of any.

Q. Then five per cent of Albert coal is enough to enrich the gas?

A. I have never used Albert coal; but I have noticed it as it has been used, and I have seen, as I stated, eight per cent sometimes used.

Q. Then a hundred pounds of Albert coal would be enough for a ton of the other coal?

A. It might; I never used it, and I may be mistaken.

Q. How much coke would a ton of coal produce? Won't it produce about fifty bushels?

A. I am trying to ascertain that by measuring very carefully this year.

Q. Can you answer it approximately?

A. I don't think so. I use now nearly fifty per cent; some parties claim that twenty-five per cent of all the coke they make will furnish all the heat that is necessary for the carbonizing of coals, and for their boilers. I doubt it. Forty or fifty per cent, or even sixty per cent, is used at the works, and the balance is sold.

Q. I mean the absolute production of coke. You produce more than a chaldron from a ton of coal?

A. Yes, sir.

Q. You sell that chaldron for about $4.

A. Yes, sir.

Q. Do you sell any other product?

A. We try to sell the coal tar, but it is rather a drug in the market now, I am sorry to say.

Q. Do you remember the gentleman's name who addressed that inquiry to you about the propriety of laying down two sets of pipes?

A. No, sir, I do not; I have forgotten it.

Q. Do you know that that gentleman, Mr. Dean, has now become president of a competing company in Detroit?

A. I didn't know before; I know there is a competing company there, and that there has been a great war raised there.

Q. Do you know about how long ago he sent you those inquiries?

A. No, sir.

Q. He wrote you and other gentlemen as to the practicability of putting down two sets of gas pipes in the same streets. Wasn't that the substance of his inquiry?

A. Yes, sir.

Q. The occupancy of the same streets by two gas companies?

A. Yes, that was his inquiry.

Q. He went to Detroit and became president of a competing company, didn't he?

A. You say it is Mr. Dean; I believe the name is Fitch.

Q. Mr. Dean is president of the opposition company: Mr. Fitch is one of the officers. ⋆Are you a member of the American Gas Light Association?

A. Yes; I was present at the meeting.

Q. That is composed of the leading men of the different corporations, is it not?

A. Yes, sir.

Q. For what purpose?

A. For the purpose of collecting statistics and information in regard to the manufacture of gas.

Q. And helping one another?

A. Yes, helping one another.

Q. And where one of them strike, the others come in and help them?

A. No, sir, I deny that. I went to the meeting in New York, and I found there was a great deal of feeling about naphtha gas. I had no such feeling; but they were kind enough to appoint me as chairman of a committee to investigate this matter in regard to the use of petroleum for making gas. I visited the Mutual Works, the Harlem Works, and several others. I want it distinctly understood that that is the object of the association. If I knew it had any other object I would not belong to it.

Q. Have you yourself used iron or clay retorts?

A. Used clay for a great many years.

Q. Do I understand you to decline to answer how much a thousand feet it costs to produce gas?

A. I have not been asked.

Q. I will ask you then: How much gas, exactly, does a ton of coal average?

A. I think we average 4.88 to the pound; it was 4.78 last month — made, not sold.

Q. Then how much a thousand feet does the coal cost?

A. The coal costs, as I told you, just about a dollar.

Q. Then you deduct for coke 17 cents, do you not?

A. Yes, sir.

Q. How much does it cost for purifying the gas?
A. I do not keep that separate. I say wages and salaries, sixty-six cents.
Q. Does that include distribution?
A. Every thing.
Q. How much taxes do you pay?
A. Fifteen cents.
Q. How much for leakage?
A. We lost last year thirteen per cent; partly in the street lamps, I am sorry to say.
Q. Is that included in the cost?
A. I take the cost of a thousand feet sold. If I took the cost per thousand feet made, it would be much less.
Q. Is there any other element that enters into the cost of gas?
A. There is general repairs.
Q. What is made costs very much less per foot than what is sold,—you deduct your leakage?
A. Of course it does; I take exactly what is sold.
Q. How much does it cost a thousand feet for repairs?
A. Well, I put in, for all other expenses, to keep my works up, so many cents—10, 15, or 20 cents.
Q. That is included in the general charge for wages or labor?
A. No, sir; wages and labor are entirely separate. I have a great many different items; I try to boil them down.
Q. How near did you get to it; how much for repairs per thousand feet?
A. I don't think I can say that.
Q. Can't you give us an idea how much it costs you a thousand feet of gas made; not distributed?
A. I can't, because I never considered that of any consequence whatever.
Q. How much does it cost to distribute it?
A. It costs not far from $2.50, with six per cent on the capital.
Q. Adding six per cent on the capital?

A. Yes, sir. I think the works are run as close as any other; that I figure as close as anybody.

Q. Will you give the elements of that cost? How do you get it up to $2.50 per thousand?

A. Well, six per cent interest on $500,000; you can reckon that up.

Q. Are you including your dividends in the cost?

A. No, sir; no dividend. The dividend is ten per cent. I include six per cent interest, because I did that years ago and have always kept it up. The rate of dividend is not so great now as it was. I want to leave you a little in a cloud; I don't want to say exactly what it costs, because Mr. Kennedy has not, on the other side.

Q. We do not figure up quite two dollars, and would like to know where you get the other fifty cents?

A. I hope the Alderman from Charlestown will call upon me, and I can show him the books. I want to be as reticent as others. I want to stand on my dignity; I think if I do so the Aldermen will think more of me than they will if I let everything out.

Q. (By ALDERMAN POWER.) How much gas did you say you made a day?

A. We made last year 60,000,000 feet. It is rather an infant beside the Boston Gas Light Company.

Q. How much are your works capable of making?

A. They would not make much more; the capacity of the gas-holder is not sufficient. We can make 500,000 feet a day with the retort-house. The purifying-house requires to be enlarged very soon, and also the storage. The mains should also be enlarged, if we wished to send out at a fair pressure much more gas. We are now running the mains simply for the use of the city. After what happened at the State House, at which you were present, we are now running the mains simply to supply the street-lamps, in many cases, and that of course leaves us very poor property.

Q. Then your works are not capable of making much more than you are now making?

A. The retort-house is calculated for 500,000 feet. Plans are made for an extension that will enable us to make a million, but it has not been done.

Q. What is your storage capacity?

A. About 300,000 feet. We are running very close, waiting to see what the times will develop. We are not extending much now.

Q. (By MR. PUTNAM.) How much do you sell the city?

A. That I can't give you. I think my clerk told me that the amount this last month was $2,000 for the street lamps.

Q. At two dollars fifty cents?

A. Two dollars fifty cents.

Q. You did not have that arrangement with the city of Charlestown?

A. No, sir; $2.75. We charged $3.00 but I offered to let them have it for $2.75 if they would burn all night. They did a while, until we had a very economical government, and then they followed the moon.

Q. (By ALDERMAN HARRIS.) Did I understand you to say that the Boston Gas Light Company manufactures a superior quality of gas to that of your company?

A. They do; they manufacture a gas of a richer candlepower; but many of our consumers, who burn gas both sides of the line, say they like the Charlestown Company's gas better. I know the reason; it is because, when gas is rich, it is apt to smoke, unless there is a burner that is adapted to it. If our consumers are satisfied, I am. The candle-power is 16; sometimes 17, at the works.

Q. (By MR. PUTNAM.) On the whole, taking the average of consumers and the average of burners, as they stand now, which satisfies them best, 18, 19 or 20 candle power, or 16 to 18?

A. I don't know; but it is the opinion of most gas engineers, and those connected with gas companies, that a 15 or 16 candle coal gas is more acceptable to consumers than gas of a higher power.

Q. Can you explain the reasons?

A. Well, it is simply this. You take a kerosene lamp chimney, and attempt to give a greater candle power by turning it up, and it smokes; and that applies to the burners in use; many of them are not adapted to this gas that is burning here.

Q. (By ALDERMAN PETERS.) Do you think that, if you were burning gas of 15 candle power, the bill would be larger than if it was but 18 candle?

A. It would depend a great deal upon the consumers. There would hardly be, I think, that difference which Mr. Kennedy has mentioned, — 25 per cent. We could not afford to make as rich gas as is made by the Boston Gas Light Co. I do not think they could afford it the past year; I don't know why they should give away gas, or sell it for less than it costs them.

MR PUTNAM. Is not this it: that this richer gas, unless carefully watched, and used in the proper burners, smokes a great deal more, and burns with a yellower light, than people like?

A. That is what I say. They will look at our gas, and say, "What a beautiful white light! what splendid gas!"

Q. But this white light is made by poor gas?

A. Yes sir; but that is what people say, and some like it better.

Q. (By MR. COLLINS.) You say that the general conclusion to which gas engineers have come is that gas of 16 candle power is the best?

A. From 16 to 18. I do not mean to say any thing about the price.

Q. Is not that the best gas for the company?

A. They will sell more.

Q. That is, the meter will register more?

A. Of course it will.

Q. Isn't it an axiom with the manufacturers of gas, that, the heavier and richer a gas is, the slower the meter will register it?

A. A pound of feathers will weigh as much as a pound of lead; a cubic foot of rich gas will measure just the same as a cubic foot of poor gas; but a cubic foot of rich gas has more illuminating power than a cubic foot of poor gas; therefore it is not necessary to burn so much to get a given amount of light; that is the way I understand it.

Q. My question is, whether gas of 16 candle power will not go through the meter quicker than gas of 18 or 20 candle power?

A. No sir; I will give you a very good reason for saying so. All our meters are inspected by the State Inspector, with air, which is a very poor gas indeed; and those same meters are stamped, approved, and sent out, and we measure the gas that is burned by them.

Q. It amounts to the same thing in the end. A person burning 20 candle gas for one month will pay less than a person burning 16 candle gas, using the same number of burners?

A. He would pay less because he would get a better light. That is true.

Q. (By Mr. Morse.) But the meters will register the same amount?

A. Just the same amount.

Q. (By Mr. Collins.) If the meters will register the same amount, then they will pay just the same if the gas is the same price per thousand feet.

A. If this were a very rich gas, 40 or 50 candle power, they could not keep it up.

Q. I understood your answer to the question of Mr. Morse to be, that if you are burning a 20 candle gas in this burner, and 16 candle gas in that, or if you take four of these burners, and are burning 16 candle gas in one chandelier, and 20 in the other, and you have a meter here, and a meter there, at the end of the month you will have to pay for as many thousand feet of the 20 candle gas as of the 16?

A. If you have the same aperture fully open, you will

pay exactly the same, whether the gas is lighter or heavier. If the gas blows, it is too rich, and I turn it down; I save in that way.

Q. You get as much light for less money?

A. Yes, sir, that is true.

Q. (By MR. PUTNAM.) By using less gas?

A. It is the use of the thumb and finger that does the business.

On motion of Alderman Peters, the further consideration of this subject was postponed until Monday afternoon, Nov. 30, at half-past four o'clock.

III.

HEARING

BEFORE THE BOARD OF ALDERMEN

ON THE

PETITION OF CITIZENS' GAS LIGHT CO.,

NOV. 30, 1874.

Nov. 30, 1874.

The hearing was resumed at half-past four.

Alderman Bigelow and Alderman Worthington presented sundry petitions in support of the petition of the Citizens' Gas Light Company.

TESTIMONY OF WILLIAM W. GREENOUGH.

Q. (By Mr. Morse). Mr. Greenough, will you state what is your relation to the Boston Gas Light Company?

A. I am Agent and Treasurer of the Boston Gas Light Company.

Q. And for how long a time have you been?

A. Twenty-two years.

Q. How long has the company itself been organized?

A. The company itself was organized in 1822. The first company failed; and their charter and property were sold, in 1824, to Cyrus Alger of South Boston, who re-sold those two properties, in 1827, to Henry Robinson and others, who formed the present Boston Gas Light Comany. It was re-organized some time in 1836, and from that time up to the present has retained precisely the same form of organization.

Q. What portion of the present city limits does the Boston Gas Light Company supply?

A. The Boston Gas Light Company supplies now the city proper alone. The pipes formerly went as far as the Norfolk House in Roxbury; but on the formation of the Roxbury Gas Light Company, the Boston Gas Light Company sold its mains to the Roxbury Gas Light Company, who now use them, and supply gas to that portion of the city.

Q. Are you able to state what is the amount of capital invested by all the gas-light companies which now supply different parts of the city? If so, will you please state it?

A. The city of Boston is now supplied by seven gas companies within its limits, and one without: the Charlestown Company, with a capital of five hundred thousand dollars; the Roxbury Company, with a capital of six hundred thousand dollars; the Jamaica Plain Company, with a capital of a hundred and seventy-three thousand dollars; the South Boston Company, with a capital of four hundred and forty thousand dollars; the East Boston Company, with a capital of two hundred and twenty thousand dollars; the Dorchester Company, with a capital of four hundred thousand dollars, — making a total of two million three hundred and thirty-three thousand dollars. Add to that the capital of the Boston Gas Light Company, two million five hundred thousand dollars, and you have four million eight hundred and thirty-three thousand dollars invested in the manufacture of gas in Boston, without taking into consideration the Brookline Company, which supplies Brighton. They are unable to say what proportion of their capital is employed in supplying Brighton; they have, however, three hundred and fifty thousand dollars capital invested.

Q. Does that all represent money paid in?

A. That all represents money paid in, so far as I know.

Q. Can you state the number of miles of street mains of all the companies?

A. In order that the Board may fully understand the matter, I will state that there are in Boston proper 120 miles of public and private streets; in South Boston, $38\frac{1}{2}$ miles; in East Boston, $35\frac{1}{2}$ miles; in Roxbury, 60 miles; in Dorchester, 69 miles; in West Roxbury, 85 miles; in Brighton, 28 miles; and in Charlestown, 28 miles, — making a total of 464 miles of public and private streets in the city of Boston.

In those streets there are laid 260 miles of gas mains. In Boston proper, which was the first precinct that I read, there are 120 miles of public and private streets, in which there are, at the present time, 105 miles of gas main. That does not, however, indicate that all but 15 miles of the streets, lanes, and by-ways are supplied with gas mains, because a great many of the mains are laid in duplicate, in some cases in triplicate, and in quadruplicate in some streets; of course, there is a considerable number of back steeets, lanes, and places where there are no mains laid. In South Boston there are 21 miles of street mains laid to 38 miles in the whole; in Roxbury, 48 miles to 60 in the whole; in Jamaica Plain, 18 miles out of 85; in East Boston, 10 miles out of 35; in Dorchester, 33 miles out of 69. These gas companies in Charlestown, Roxbury, Jamaica Plain, South Boston, East Boston, and Dorchester made in the year 1873, 260,309,000 cubic feet of gas. In Boston proper, the Boston Gas Light Company made 668,210,000. Of those two amounts, there were sold out of the city proper, 230,731,000, and in Boston proper, 612,000,000; making the total amount of gas lost and unaccounted for, out of the city, 29,000,000 cubic feet, and in the city, 56,000,000 cubic feet; or a total of 85,000,000 feet of gas unaccounted for; the whole amount of the loss being a little less than ten per cent, which is about the average loss in the best conducted companies in the world. The street lamps supplied by these gas companies I have not a full account of, Jamaica Plain being wanting in my statement; that, however, is probably given in some books which are in the Aldermen's hands; but the total number of street lights out of the city proper, exclusive of Jamaica Plain, is 3,687, and 3,828 in Boston proper; making a total of 7,515 public lights supplied by the gas companies.

The number of meters which they have in Charlestown, is 3980; in Roxbury, 3975; in Jamaica Plain, 650; South Boston, 2026; East Boston, 1200; Dorchester, 900; making a total of 12,731 outside of Boston proper; and

22,708 in Boston proper; making a total of 35,639 meters in use in the city of Boston.

Q. Going back to your own company, will you state what has been the policy of the company in respect to going into new strets, laying supplies, furnishing meters, and making repairs?

A. The policy of the company was substantially adopted many years since; in fact, before I became associated with it. In regard to the laying of mains in the streets, we have always, or nearly always, preceded consumption, so that there has been no request ever made of us, except in two or three instances, to lay mains in any public street.

Q. Has the company waited, before going into a street, until the amount of consumption would pay for the expense of laying pipes there?

A. It has not. It has always looked to the general interest; to the probable condition of the population; and, when the company saw that streets were likely to be settled, they put their mains in; the street-lamps were put there, and consumption followed in the course of time.

Q. Has the company ever made any charge for the supplies?

A. It never has.

Q. Or for meters?

A. It has never made any charge for meters. In its early history, I think in 1828, and from that on to 1836, meter-rents were charged; but they were given up, I think, in 1836, and supplies were put in without charge, as I before observed.

Q. How is it in regard to repairs?

A. The Boston Gas Light Company is the only gaslight company in the world, so far as I am aware, which keeps a body of men in its service, whose duty it is to attend to the complaints of consumers; that is, when a man's gas does not burn, if any thing is the matter with his house distribution, any thing the matter with his meter, he is at liberty always to send to the office, and people are sent to answer the complaint, and to answer any inquiry, without charge. That is done nowhere else, that I know of, in the world.

Q. What system does the company have in respect to meeting these demands? Are your men on hand all the time?

A. Yes, sir; by day and night. There is a corps of men who remain in the office through the regular office-hours, and there are men who are there at night, to answer all calls. There are usually three or four men who sleep in the office, whose business it is to attend to any sort of complaint.

Q. Please describe now the method of determining the illuminating power of gas.

A. That is done by an instrument called a photometer, in which the light of the gas is measured by the light of a candle. By general acceptation, in England and in this country, the standard candle, burning 120 grains to the hour, is taken as the standard of measure for the value of gas.

The lights are placed opposite to one another, and between them is a screen, consisting of a piece of greased paper, and this paper is moved between the two lights until no shadow is cast upon it, so that the light of the gas is precisely the light of the candle; and, as the value of the light is as the square of the distance, it is very easily calculated what the candle-power of the gas is. By modern contrivances, the photometers are adjusted so that the scale which is before you measures precisely the value of the light; and then, having weighed the candle, you see how much of it has burned, and reduce it to the standard of 120 grains to the hour. It is not an entirely satisfactory process, but it is the best which has obtained yet in England or in this country. The reason I say it is unsatisfactory is this: because it is almost impossible to obtain two candles which shall burn precisely the same amount, giving the same amount of light. Of course, the larger amount of sperm they consume, the more light they give in proportion. The French system is much better, but it has not been adopted generally in England or in this country; and, when we talk about gas, we must have a measure which everybody knows. So, when we talk about 16 or 18 candle power gas, we mean, that, when compared with a candle burning 120 grains an hour, the light of the gas is equal to 16 or 18 candles, as the case may be.

Q. Is it possible to tell by the sight alone the illuminating power of gas?

A. I should say not. I have had pretty long experience. The condition of the eye depends, as gentlemen know, very much upon the condition of the stomach, and that is hardly twice alike in any man.

Q. What is the average illuminating power of the Boston Gas Light Co.'s gas?

A. The average illuminating power, I should say, was between $18\frac{1}{2}$ and 19 candles; you mean at the present time, or for a series of years?

Q. I will ask, at the present time?

A. I should say that for a series of years it has been so.

Q. Is that a cheaper or dearer gas to the consumer than 16 or 17 candles?

A. Cheaper gas.

Q. And why?

A. Because one has to burn a less amount to get the amount of light required for convenience; that is, as Prof. Rogers testified in a hearing before a committee of the city government, some years ago, the eye measures for itself the amount of light which it requires, and the burner is usually adjusted to give about the light of 16 candles, as being the most agreeable light to the eye, and, of course, if you are burning five cubic feet of gas, and it gives the light of 20 candles, then the burner is turned down, so that less shall be burned, — sufficient to give the light of 16 candles, or whatever the individual wants.

Q. Your company makes its gas entirely from coal, does it?

A. It does.

Q. What kind of coal?

A. We use the most expensive sorts of coal which are used in the United States by any gas company; necessarily, in the first place, on account of our position; because so large a portion of our coal comes through southern cities — comes through Philadelphia, Baltimore, and Richmond. Of course the expense of transportation makes that coal cost much more than it does in those seaport towns from which it comes, because there is always transportation by sea to be added to the cost of the coal in the city from which it is shipped. The most costly coal we use is the Albert coal — the coal upon which the illuminating power of our gas mainly depends.; that is, its illuminating power over and above the common standard. This coal is mined in New Brunswick, and costs us about $25.00 in gold here. Of course, where so large an amount of coal is required as we use, quite a number of varieties are purchased, as we cannot rely upon any one kind to give us absolutely the coal we require. We use the Penn coal, from western Pennsylvania; we use the Youghiogheny coal from the same region, from the Youghiogheny river; we use also some of the coals which are shipped from Baltimore, differing from year to year, according as the grade seems to be better. This year we had a coal shipped from Baltimore, called the Monongahela coal; then from Richmond we have had shipped, this year, from the new mines now opening in West Virginia, a few thousand tons of the West Virginia coals — quite superior coals for gas-making purposes. We also receive a certain amount from the Provinces, — Cape Breton, and Pictou coal, — less in amount than formerly.

Q. What are the freights from Baltimore and Philadelphia to Boston?

A. Taking the average of years, they would be about $2.50 from Philadelphia, and, perhaps, $2.75 from Baltimore. This year they have been cheaper than that.

Q. Is there any addition to the cost, besides the freight

on the Pennsylvania coal, here, over and above the price in Philadelphia?

A. Only the price of the freights.

Q. There is that difference, of course?

A. There is that difference. In Richmond, there is a little difference in addition to that, the cost of transhipment, which is a few cents a ton.

Q. How is the cost of coal here as compared with that in New York?

A. Higher.

Q. There is a process of purification used in the manufacture of gas; is there not?

A. All crude gas requires to be purified before it can be delivered for consumption.

Q. What is the object of purifying it?

A. The object of purifying is to take from it the offensive matters which it contains, — take from it the sulphur, ammonia, and carbonic acid.

Q. What have you used for the purpose of purifying gas?

A. We use wet and dry lime.

Q. Is there any substitute as good as that that you know of?

A. There is nothing so perfect in its operation as lime. There are other forms of purification which are in use, especially having reference to the removal of the sulphur. Certain companies trust very much to their washing to remove the ammonia from the gas, and trust to the oxide of iron purification for the removal of sulphur; sometimes they are united. There is a patented process in England which unites lime and oxide of iron to remove the three impurities, — sulphur, ammonia, and carbonic acid.

Q. Have you given some consideration to the question of the substitution of naphtha for high-priced coals?

A. Not a great deal. It has been brought to my attention by a large number of inventors and patentees, who come to assure you that their invention is no longer an experiment, but a distinguished success; but I have never felt inclined to try the process at all. I never believed in it.

Q. Where are the objections to it?

A. Well, sir, in the first place, the quantity of naphtha which we should be obliged to use would be so large that I doubt whether the Board of Aldermen would allow us to place anywhere in the city such a quantity.

Q. What would be the quantity necessary to keep?

A. It would differ according to the different processes; but I am sure the Board of Aldermen would not allow me to put ten thousand barrels of gunpowder anywhere in Boston, even if I assured them, upon my word of honor, that it should never explode, and that the apparatus which covered it was free from danger; and yet naphtha is a far more dangerous compound than gunpowder, and I should be very loath to come to the Board of Aldermen, and ask them for any such leave. I don't think that I could offer any guaranty which would be satisfactory to them.

Q. As far as you can form an estimate, what quantity of naphtha would be required by either one of the processes which you know of, for a winter's supply in Boston?

A. Well, by the only process which I have particularly examined, I think the quantity required was from ten to twenty thousand barrels. That would be from two to three months' stock. Of course, in the winter, we must have a supply of manufacturing material beyond all question.

Q. Now, in reference to the quantity of gas that may be made from coal, will you state what is the average product that is made from coal?

A. In order to explain that, I, perhaps, should give some little explanation to the Board of the process of manufacture. I dare say it is sufficiently familiar to all, that the process consists of charging heated retorts with coal, closing the mouths, and letting the gas pass through the hydraulic main into the purifying and distributing apparatus. The quantity of the gas taken from a pound of coal depends upon the heating of the retort. The object of the gas engineer is to get the largest amount of good gas from his coal; not the largest amount of gas, but the largest amount of *good* gas. Different coals, of course, yield different quantities of the best gas that they produce. Some coals yield only three and a half feet to the pound of sixteen-candle gas. The same coal, if worked at a high heat, would yield from four to four and a half feet to the pound; but it would be very poor gas; of course, the larger the quantity of gas, the poorer the quality. It has been for many years the object of engineers and scientific men to see if this quantity of gas, made from a pound of coal, the legitimate product of the coal at a regular heat, could be strengthened; that is, the quality kept up, and the quantity increased; and that probably is the cause of many of these patents, which are before the public, for giving a large amount of gas at a low price, and claimed to be gas of good quality; the best American coals yield, of their best grade, about four and a half feet to the pound; that is, about 10,000 feet to the ton.

Q. Have you made an examination, to ascertain the actual receipts from the sale of gas, coke, and coal tar by the company during the last year?

A. I have.

Q. Won't you state what they were?

A. In order to make this entirely intelligible to the Board, I will state it in two ways, taking as the basis of calculation the total amount of our sales of gas, coke, and coal tar, less the cost of production, office expenses, and repairs actually made; less the losses by bad debts, we have a profit of 26½ cents on each thousand feet sold, which is less than 10 per cent upon the capital; 10 per cent on the capital amounting to a little less than 30 cents.

Q. Perhaps it would be more intelligible if you would state what was the amount of capital last year?

A. The amount of capital was two millions.
Q. So that 10 per cent upon that would be $200,000?
A. Yes, sir.
Q. 610,000,000 was the amount sold by the company?
A. 612,000,000.
Q. And the amount of profit was 26½ cents on each thousand feet?
A. Yes.
Q. That, you say, is less than 10 per cent upon the $2,000,000?
A. Yes, sir, upon the capital.
Q. Now, can you state the actual amounts received from the sales?
A. The sales, exclusive of coke and coal tar, were $1,490,537.70; inclusive of coke and coal tar, $1,602,600.13; that is $2.39 per thousand, on the whole amount of gas sold. The cost was $1,393,869.53, or $2.08 per thousand. That is, however, exclusive of bad debts; add 4½ cents for those, and you have $2.12½ per thousand.
Q. The actual cost this last year, you say, was $2.08, without taking into account bad debts?
A. Yes, sir.
Q. And, making the proper discount for bad debts, you have $2.12½?
A. Yes, sir.
Q. (By ALDERMAN PETERS.) Do you include in this any expense for laying pipes?
A. No.
Q. (By MR. MORSE.) Won't you state what are the elements in the cost made up there?
A. Coal, labor at the works, purification, fire-brick, retorts, gas expenses, carting and repairs, repairing street mains, office labor, public lights, taxes, expenses, loss by leakage, bad debts, no interest on capital.
Q. Then, as the result from that, Mr. Greenough, were the profits of the company last year sufficient to pay 10 per cent upon the capital?

A. They were not.

Q. (By ALDERMAN PETERS.) Did you allow any thing in that for the expense of laying pipes in the burnt district?

A. That is not included at all.

Q. (By MR. MORSE.) I wish to make that clear, whether there was any thing included there which was any special expense growing out of the fire?

A. No, sir, there is nothing in it; neither the street mains, nor the meters, nor the services that were necessary to rehabilitate the burnt district.

Q. Will you state, by the way, to what expense the company went, last year, in furnishing new meters, supplies, &c.?

A. I can not state from memory; but it was quite large.

Q. At all events, all the expenses growing out of the fire, the loss of meters, the supply-pipes, and so on, you have had to make good, last year and this year?

A. We have.

Q. But that does not enter into the elements of cost which you have stated here?

A. No.

Q. Let me ask, in passing, what was done in reference to the accounts due for gas, at the time of the fire, in the burnt district; were those collected?

A. They were not. No charge was made of the amount of gas consumed by the quarterly consumers from the first of October to the ninth of November, 1872.

Q. Now, in reference to the cost and the price of gas during the present year, are you able to determine, as yet, what the relation of one to the other is?

A. Not until the accounts are made up at the end of the year.

Q. Can you form now a judgment as to the price at which the gas can be sold during the coming year?

A. Not yet.

Q. When will that be determined?

A. Not until the accounts are made up, which will probably be in the month of March. I say in the month of March, because you must be aware that making up the accounts of a large corporation like ours, with a great many accounts, occupies a great deal of time. We have a trial-balance, which occupies the whole time of two very efficient clerks during the year, and that trial-balance is usually finished the last of February or first of March. When that is done the accounts can be made up.

Q. Before leaving this question of receipts, will you explain to the Board the price which the company actually receives from the sale of gas. The price to the original consumer is $2.50 per thousand; what is it to the wholesale consumer?

A. There is 5 per cent discount to the city on gas burned by meter. People consuming over a thousand dollars' worth a year have 5 per cent discount allowed. Then, for the street-lamps, we have, as I stated the other evening, $2.08 per thousand feet.

Q. So that, if I understand your figures, although the price is ordinarily spoken of as $2.50 a thousand, the actual receipt of the company is on the average $2.39, or was last year?

A. In 1873 the average receipts were $2.39.

Q. Will you state, now, in regard to the present condition of the company, what amount of property the company owns that is invested and used in the manufacture and distribution of gas?

A. Well, sir, that may be stated in two ways: in the first place, what it stands at upon the books of the company; and, secondly, the valuation which the city gives to it for purposes of taxation. To-day the capital stock of the company is 2½ millions. On the first of July, there was a surplus of $380,000, also invested in this business; making a total of $2,880,000 which is invested in the business; of which $2,500,000 has to pay dividends. In the year 1873 the capital was $2,000,000 invested in the business. We had a surplus something less, — I have forgotten now. The surplus was a little more at the end of the year 1872 than in July, 1873, four, five, or six thousand dollars, perhaps. The property taxed to the corporation, by the city, was something over $3,400,000. Of course this property, whatever the value was, was earning a dividend simply upon $2,000,000; so that it was of no sort of value to the corporation that its property was worth so much more than it had cost. It simply stood upon its books at what it cost, and was only earning for the corporation interest on its original cost.

Q. So that, to compare the Boston Company with the New York Company spoken of here, that company, with a nominal capital of five millions, but only two and a half millions paid in, would have to earn dividends upon five millions, although it had only half as much as that in the way of property; whereas your company earn dividends upon two millions, having actually invested property to a considerable amount in excess of that?

A. Yes.

Q. So that the cost would be less to the consumer of the gas of your company than of the other company, would it not?

A. It works in two ways; in the first place, it makes property more permanent; and, secondly, it gives to the consumer the advantage of any increase of the capital put into the business, upon which no dividend is paid.

Q. Is a portion of your property real estate which has risen in value?

A. A very considerable portion. We have in the city proper between eleven and twelve acres of land distributed in the various wards of the city; the larger portion of it in Ward 2; but we also have property in Wards 3, 6, 7, 11, 13 and 16. All this real estate is occupied for the purposes of the company, and I believe that we occupy less land than any other large gas company in the world, doing the same amount of business.

Q. You find it necessary to occupy eleven acres?

A. Eleven acres. I should say, also, that we have purchased an additional tract of territory at Dorchester, upon deep water, at Commercial Point, for the purpose of building, at some future day, another station, another set of works. We have there about twenty acres.

Q. Does the company own and have pipes, and other appliances, sufficient to supply the city of Boston within the limits that its charter authorizes it to?

A. It has, of course, because it is supplying the city. Do you mean for the future?

Q. Yes, sir, for the prospective increase of the city.

A. Of course, a gas company must always be before its work. It must anticipate demand; so that our works, at the present time, without any addition to them, would probably take care of the city for another winter, or possibly two winters; so with the works in the process of construction in Dorchester, the gas-holder now built will take care of the consumption for another winter or two winters.

Q. What I mean is, whether there is need of another gas company in order to supply this territory which you cover?

A. I don't see that there is the slightest.

Q. Something has been said in reference to the large quantities of coke that are made in the manufacture of gas. Do you use a portion of the coke in your manufacture?

A. A portion of the coke is used in the manufacture. In a series of years, taking the rise and fall of coke, as compared with other articles of fuel, the coke that is sold usually brings about 10 per cent of the cost of the coal.

Q. How does the price of coke here compare with that in Pittsburg, for instance?

A. I am not able to speak positively about that, but the value of coke in Pittsburg is larger than the value of coal, because it is much in demand for manufacturing iron. In England, it is the same way. Good coke, through almost the whole of England, sells for more than coal.

Q. You spoke in your testimony in regard to a large and unaccountable difference between the amount of your manufacture and the amount of gas sold; what is the meaning of that?

A. Through the better managed gas companies in the world, having an extended distribution, 10 per cent is thought to be the amount of gas which should be unaccounted for; that is, gas which is lost by leakage, or condensation, or stealage, — leakage and condensation being, of course, the two principal causes of disappearance of gas.

Q. Something, also, has been stated about retorts; what kind of retorts do you use?

A. We use a certain number of iron retorts, and a certain number of clay retorts. Most of the companies in the United States use clay retorts alone. We use iron retorts for the purpose of carbonizing our Albert coal, which requires a different treatment from the ordinary coals, keeping up the grade of our gas as high as we possibly can from the coals which we use.

Q. Which costs most, iron, or clay retorts?

A. Iron. Iron retorts cost more for two reasons: one, for the first cost; secondly, for the duration. Ordinarily, iron retorts do not last much more than half the time of ordinary clay retorts.

Q. But you find it necessary to use iron with the Albert coal?

A. So long as we continue to carbonize Albert coal, I suppose we shall be obliged to use iron retorts.

Q. Have you had some sketches prepared which show the condition of the city as to pipes?

A. I have, sir.

Q. Won't you please explain those to the Board of Aldermen?

A. The question of taking up the streets of Boston is a very different consideration from that which obtains any where else in this country. This plan, which is upon the floor, shows the location of the sewer, gas, and water pipes, and horse-railroad tracks, on Tremont and Washington Street, between Scollay's Square and Pleasant Street.

[The witness explained various plans which he had caused to be prepared, showing the situation of the various pipes in the streets.] *

Q. Have you given some attention to the matter of competition of gas companies in other cities?

A. I have, sir.

Q. Will you state to the Board what has been the history of competition of gas companies in other cities, as far as you know it?

A. I do not know of any competing gas company that has ever earned a dividend. I have here in my hand a memorandum with regard to the city of Brooklyn, where there are various gas companies supplying separate districts. The old Brooklyn Co. commenced business in '49; the Citizens' Co. in '61, and for two years the Citizens' Co. were in competition with the old Brooklyn Co. The old company met the new company by putting down the price of their gas to 12½ cents per thousand in every street where the new company laid their mains. At the end of two years, that competition was sufficient; and the Citizens' Co. bought a district of the old Brooklyn Co. I have here a map of Brooklyn, divided into gas districts, showing how six companies now supply what was originally supplied by two; that is, the Williamsburg Co. and the old Brooklyn Co. [Map exhibited.] This matter, of course, is a pretty old one. The question came up in London many years ago.

Q. Before you leave Brooklyn, I will ask you if the price of gas in Brooklyn is any less at the present time than it was before the competition.

A. It remains at $3.00 per thousand, $2.50 for the public lights.

Q. There was competition lasting two years, and then the companies divided the city?

---

* The large plan referred to in Mr. Greenough's testimony has not been reproduced for this volume, on account of its great size. The other plans have been reproduced, and are inserted at beginning of book.

A. No. The Brooklyn Company sold a district to the Citizens' Company, as I understand. In London, — I don't know as I can fix exactly the year, but previous to 1858, — the city was supplied by thirteen companies; and through some of the great streets of London there ran several lines of street main belonging to different companies. In 1858, I myself saw a trench opened in the Strand, which exposed the mains of four different companies which passed through that part of the Strand. The great inconvenience of this compelled the companies to re-arrange their districts. They were continually tapping one another's pipes. Whenever a leak occurred, there was a quarrel between the companies as to whose main the leak was in. This company declined to dig; and another company declined to dig; and there was the greatest possible confusion, and great leakage of gas, throughout the city. They then districted the city, each company keeping its own district for a number of years, until, by an act of Parliament, some of the larger companies were allowed to purchase some of the smaller ones; and now the Imperial Co. and the Chartered Co., which are two of the great companies, mainly supply London. There are other large companies, but none so large as these two. The Imperial Gas Light Co. and the Chartered Co. both have works in progress a few miles out of London, by which they can manufacture and supply between ten and twenty million cubic feet of gas a day each.

Q. Is there any competition in London now?
A. None at all.
Q. The city is divided into districts?
A. The city is divided into districts.
Q. Although there has been competition?
A. There has been competition in former years.
Q. To the extent of several companies?
A. To the extent of several companies running pipes through the same district. In Paris, the case was different: the government there interposed. There were eight

companies, some in competition, and others supplying districts; but the Emperor Napoleon, having made up his mind that something must be done to bring the gas distribution of Paris to a system, had an exploration made by men of science, in a special retort house, of the cost of gas, and the processes by which gas is made, and then offered to the companies in Paris, if they would unite, and form one company, under one head, to grant a concession to that company of the supply of gas to Paris for fifty years. That was done; and the great Parisian company has gone on from that time supplying solely the entire city of Paris.

Q. That ended the competition?

A. That ended the competition. In some of the larger continental cities there are two companies, but none in the same districts, that I am aware of. At Amsterdam, Berlin, and St. Petersburg, there are two companies, in Stockholm one, in Hamburg one.

Q. Those are not competing companies?

A. No, not competing companies. In this country we have the example of New York before us. New York covers 22,000 acres, and has about 250 miles of streets (I think that can hardly be right). It is supplied by five companies, — the New York, with a capital of $4,000,000; the Manhattan, with a capital of $4,000,000; the Metropolitan, with a capital of $2,500,000; the Harlem, with a capital of $1,800,000; and the New York Mutual, with a capital of $5,000,000. Those companies, in the aggregate, made, in 1873, about 3,600,000,000 cubic feet of gas. The capital invested in the city of New York is $17,300,000. The meaning of that is, of course, that, if those companies pay ten per cent dividends, that would amount in a year to $1,730,000, which would be 48 cents per thousand cubic feet of gas made. That is, they must earn 48 cents per thousand cubic feet made to pay ten per cent dividends. On the amount of gas sold, it would amount to $54\frac{6}{10}$ cents per thousand cubic feet. The number of miles of pipe which they have laid in New York is given in this table, which will show the difference of supply there and here. I have here the lamp tables which are contained in the report of the department of public works in New York. It does not state the whole number of miles of streets. The whole number of miles laid by the New York Mutual Gas Company, to April, 1873, was 48; by the Metropolitan, 110; by the Harlem, 82; by the New York Gas Light Company, 130; by the Manhattan, 171 miles. I give these figures because they serve as a comparison with our figures here in Boston, and may be of importance to you.

Q. What is the cost of gas in New York to the consumer?

A. The price to the consumer is $2.75 per thousand. The cost of the street-lights was given, I think, the other night, at $37 or $38 per light.

Q. Is there any other city, besides New York and Detroit, where competition has been tried in this country?

A. I think it was tried at Buffalo, at St. Louis, and at some of the interior towns; also at Memphis and Chicago.

Q. Now it is stated, that in Detroit the price of gas has been reduced since this competing company went into operation; will you state to the Board your opinion as to the future continuance of that low price?

A. It is simply a matter of endurance on the part of the companies until one or the other fails; or, what is most likely to be done, as has always been done in such previous cases, when they have injured one another all they can, they combine, and fix a price by which both can live.

Q. Can the companies afford to sell gas in Detroit at the price for which they are now selling it?

A. No, sir; not at all.

Q. Do they get back even the cost of making it?

A. I should think not half the cost.

Q. You heard the estimates given by Mr. Kennedy

the other evening in reference to the price at which gas could be made, in his judgment, out of coal, of as good quality as the gas furnished by the Boston Gas Light Company. He stated that it could be made at a cost of $1.50 and sold at $2 per thousand, so as to make a fair profit to the stockholders. Will you give your opinion in regard to those estimates?

A. Mr. Kennedy, if I understood him correctly, testified that coal gas of as good or better quality than that made by the Boston Gas Light Company, can be made for $1.50 per thousand feet, and sold for $2, with a capital of $2,000,000 employed in the business, and selling 300,000,000 a year. Ten per cent per annum upon $2,000,000 of capital would be $200,000, to pay which it would be necessary to earn 66⅔ cents upon every thousand feet of gas sold. That, of course, is to be added to his $1.50, and he can hardly sell his gas at $2 and make a handsome profit. In 1873 the Boston Gas Light Company sold over 600,000,000 feet, upon which it was necessary to earn 30 cents per 1000. Or, take it the other way, suppose the two companies supply the city together, the Citizens' Compamy having a capital of $2,000,000, and the Boston Gas Light Company, having a capital of $2,500,000, and dividing the business, with its natural increase, amounting, we will say, to 800,000,000 cubic feet a year, they must each make 56 cents per thousand feet to live and prosper. I do not think this result would give " cheap gas."

Q. Were there any elements entering into the cost of gas which, in your judgment, should be added to Mr. Kennedy's statement?

A. I can't tell, of course, what were included in some of the details given by Mr. Kennedy. Take the cost of common coal at seventy-five cents per thousand feet, and Cannel coal at twenty cents, you have a total for coal of ninety-five cents per thousand feet; deducting the coke and tar, twenty-three cents, you will have seventy-two cents as the net cost of the coal. The net cost of the coal which we used in the year 1873, was eighty-seven cents, deducting coke and coal-tar, which is fifteen cents more than the sum given by Mr. Kennedy. Then, with regard to labor, he estimates labor at twenty-five cents per thousand feet. I do not know what he includes in that item. One gas company includes simply the labor of making the gas in the item of labor; others include the labor that is done about the works as part of the labor, and so on. He gives twenty-five cents as the cost. In 1873 our labor cost us fifty cents. There is a difference on those two items of coal and labor, of forty cents; so that we have $1.37 for those two items alone.

Q. In your judgment, would it be possible for any company to manufacture gas, and sell it at a profit, at $2 per thousand feet, of the same quality as your gas, made from coal.

A. No, sir; in my judgment, it cannot be done. From coal of the same grade, the gas we make could not, in my judgment, be made and sold at $2 per thousand feet, or any thing like it.

Q. If there is anything that occurs to you to add to your statement, you may add it, if you please?

A. The other evening, the counsel for the petitioners, Mr. Collins, read a list of hotels, and so on, supplied by the Mutual Gas Light Company in New York. I happened to be in New York a few days ago, and I obtained from the Manhattan Company a list of the hotels which they supply, in the same district through which the pipes of the Mutual Company are laid, showing quite a large number of important places.

[This list was handed to the Chairman without being read.]

Q. In regard to the estimate made by Mr. Kennedy as to the cost of land and buildings, street-mains, and so on: he stated, as I understood, that he allowed $1,000,000 for the cost of land and buildings, and $1.000,000 for 100 miles of street-mains, supplies, and so on.

A. Of course, every one knows the peculiar condition of the land in and about Boston. The cheap lands in the neighborhood of Boston are lands which are still to be raised to grade, and more or less recovered from the sea. Five acres of land in one block, within a reasonable distance from Boston, and at grade, I should think, could hardly be purchased for less than $1 a foot, and I do not know that they could be even for that. The estimate with regard to the cost of street-mains, and so on, I can only approximate in this way, that if large mains are laid, if the whole distribution takes place in proportion to the supply for the whole city, and the districts which are near to the city, of course the mains must be large, and the cost of distribution increased proportionately. As the gentleman said the other night, mains may cost $3,000 a mile, or $30,000 a mile. The distribution of the Boston Gas Light Company has cost about $1,000,000.

Q. Would not the expense of removing the pavement, the horse-railroad tracks, and other obstructions of that kind, add very largely to the cost of laying pipes through the city now?

A. Of course, the expense increases from year to year.

Q. I mean, if a new company were to come into the streets in their present condition, and lay pipes, would not the cost be very much more than it was in the beginning?

A. It would cost a percentage more, of course.

Q. What would be your judgment as to the effect upon other pipes in the streets, — the water-pipes, the present gas-pipes, and the sewers?

A. It would depend very much upon the level at which those pipes were laid down. The present gas mains occupy the three-feet level; that is, the tops of the mains are laid three feet below the ground, that being about the point to which frost penetrates in solid, original soil in our climate. The water-pipes, being laid subsequently to the gas-pipes, were laid upon a lower level; they took the four-feet level, and the sewers are mainly below that. Of course, another company coming into the same streets, may elect to take either a shallower or deeper level than the other gas companies, or the water-pipes; or they may elect to run at the same grade, and take care of the crossings of the other mains. I mean by that, that at the junction of every street where the pipes are united, and in the mains coming into those streets, they must go under or over the pipe which is laid on the same plane. They can go over by laying a goose-neck, or go under by reversing the gooseneck; in which case there will be a deposit of condensation, and it would be necessary to have a syphon-box to collect this material for every pipe of that sort put down. I do not know that it is possible to get a regular circulation where two sets of mains are laid upon the same grade; that is, for the second set. Of course the loosening of the soil in the streets is prejudicial to the underground work already laid. Whenever a new sewer is placed in the streets, whenever the water-pipes are altered, it is always attended with considerable expense to the Boston Gas Light Company, especially in the case of sewers, because the soil is never returned in as good, solid condition as it was previously. In some streets at the South End, where sewers have been laid, they have broken our mains in from eight to twelve places, which we were required to repair afterwards at our own expense. So with water, when the water-pipes are changed or altered in any street, the chances are ten to one that several breaks will occur in our mains, on account of the settling of the ground.

Q. Is it not a fact, that the Boston Gas Light Co. has been put to great expense on account of the fact that so many pipes have been laid in new streets, on new-made land, arising from the settling of the streets?

A. On new-made land the pipes have been more or less broken in consequence of the settling of the soil. I presume the pipes laid by the Boston Gas Light Co. are the heaviest gas-pipes laid in the United States, because, with five-eighths of our city composed of made-land, we have deemed it prudent to lay the thickest and stoutest mains obtainable.

There is one other point in this connection. In comparison with what we are doing in Boston, I should be glad to call your attention to the condition of things in Philadelphia. The city government makes its own gas, under a trust. I hold in my hand the last annual report, made in January, 1874, giving the operation of the trust for the previous year. It manufactured, in the year 1873, 1,648,000,000, in round numbers, cubic feet of gas, of which 279,000,000 were consumed in the public lights, 1,217,000,000 by private consumers, and 151,000,000 used at the offices of the trust, and lost by leakage, — they combine the use at the works and the offices of the trust with leakage. They supply 9469 public lamps, and they have mains in their streets amounting in the aggregate to 3,194,741 feet. The total number of consumers of gas in Philadelphia is 79,477. The amount invested in the works is $7,841,702. They purchased from the private owners the works at Spring Garden, Moyamensing, West Philadelphia, and Frankfort, so that the total cost of the whole works has been $11,126,161. In that statement which I have read, it is shown that the amount charged for street-lights in Philadelphia is $55.50 each per annum.

Q. (By ALDERMAN HALL.) Is that the cost of the gas, independent of lighting and repairs?

A. It does not state; it probably pays for lighting and care also. Comparing that with the same service in the city of Boston, the street-lights cost $34.68 for the gas, and $5.64 for lighting and keeping in order; making a total cost, per lamp, of about $40.

CROSS-EXAMINATION.

Q. (By MR. HYDE.) If I understood you, you said that the gas of the Boston Gas Light Co., for the year 1873, cost them $2.08 per thousand?

A. Yes.

Q. Have you the items which make up the aggregate of $2.08 in detail?

A. I have not got them, any further than those I have given here, — the important ones, — the cost of coal and the cost of labor.

Q. What is the cost of coal?

A. The cost of coal, deducting coke and coal-tar, was 87 cents; the cost of labor, 50 cents; making $1.37.

Q. How does your coal cost you 87 cents? What does your coal cost you a ton?

A. That was the average cost of all the qualities we use.

Q. You said that the cost of Albert coal was $25 a ton, what does your other coal cost you?

A. The Penn coal cost, in 1873, about $9.50 a ton. I cannot give you the exact figures; I should say, however, about $9.50 a ton.

Q. What kind of coal did you use besides Albert?

A. Penn.

Q. Is that Pennsylvania coal?

A. Yes, sir; it is Pennsylvania coal.

Q. Is that soft or hard coal?

A. Soft coal.

Q. You say that gas of as good quality as yours cannot be made for $1.50?

A. I said so.

Q. That is your judgment?

A. That is my judgment.

Q. Now, suppose there are competent parties who are investing their own capital, and are willing to undertake to make gas upon that basis of cost, how does it hurt the citizens of Boston to have the chance to buy it at that price, or with fifty cents added?

A. Well, it only hurts them in this way: that they come in and offer to make gas for $1.50 per thousand, and get admission here, and cannot do it, when they have got the streets taken up, and all that sort of thing.

Q. They put in their own capital; they do not call upon you or the city to furnish a cent; they put their own property at risk, not yours, and give me, a citizen, the right to buy gas at 50 cents a thousand less than you sell it for?

A. If you can buy as good gas as the Boston Gas Light Company makes for $1.50 a thousand, you have a right to do it.

Q. Is there any way in which I can avail myself of that privilege, unless a new company is established to do that; you don't propose to reduce the price; you propose to keep it where it is?

A. I propose to keep it where it is.

Q. If any persons are willing to come in and sell it to me and other citizens at 50 cents a thousand less, why shouldn't the city of Boston give them the privilege, and me, a citizen, the opportunity to buy it of them, if they will furnish it?

A. Of course, if any other people can come into the city and do the work better and cheaper than the Boston Gas Light Company, that company must go to the wall, that is all.

Q. Is there any reason why the same rule of competition should not apply to the supply of gas as to all other large enterprises of life?

A. Of course, that is a question for argument. It stands to reason, that two people cannot supply one household in competition with each other as well as one person can.

Q. Why would not that apply as well to all the supplies that go into a household?

A. Because that is not precisely a parallel case. With a city, with a certain number of miles of streets, and a certain number of houses on those streets, with the pipes already put down, of course a second set of pipes must be laid at an increased expense; but if people are willing to come in and take the risk of putting that second set of pipes down, and the citizens are perfectly satisfied of their ability to do what they profess to be able to do, then it is for the Board of Aldermen to take into serious consideration whether they should be permitted to do it or not.

Q. You spoke of other cities where competition has been tried; have they two competing gas companies in St. Louis?

A. I think not now.

Q. Have they had?

A. They have had, I believe.

Q. What effect did they have upon the price of gas there?

A. I can't tell you.

Q. Reduced it a dollar a thousand, didn't it?

A. I can't tell you.

Q. You have brought up the case of Detroit; is that Detroit company still going?

A. Both are going, I believe.

Q. In 1866, if I remember right, you told us the same story, that they were having a terrible time in Detroit with two gas companies, running against each other, didn't you?

A. You say so; I don't remember about that. I did if "it is so nominated in the bond." I don't know.

Q. What are the citizens of Detroit getting gas for now?

A. I believe the city lamps are supplied at thirty-seven and a half cents a thousand; it is a ridiculously low figure; they are cutting their own throats.

Q. What do the citizens pay?

A. I think about fifty cents; I don't remember.

Q. What is the largest one item that goes into the manufacture of gas?

A. Coal.

Q. Did you add labor to that cost per thousand?

A. I gave you the two principal items, — one was labor and the other coal.

Q. Now, you heard the statement made here as to the cost of gas at the Island?

A. Yes.

Q. In this estimate that you make, of course there is no interest on capital included?

A. No.

Q. There is no interest there?

A. No.

Q. Now, how can they make gas down there at a dollar a thousand or less?

A. As I understand their calculation with regard to the cost of their gas, it is simply the cost of the gas at the mouth of the retort; they simply pay for the coal from which the gas is made, and they pay nothing for their labor, except the man who has the general direction, as I understand it; so that their labor costs nothing, and they have nothing but the cost of the coal which they use.

Q. Can they manufacture in that way with nearly the economy that you can in a great concern like yours; can they manufacture an article, where only a few thousand feet are wanted, with nearly the economy with which you can manufacture it, where millions of feet are wanted?

A. It is a very different condition; we have a large and valuable apparatus.

Q. But your apparatus produces a great deal more?

A. Our apparatus produces more; but our apparatus must be so large and perfect as to be, so far as practicable, beyond the reach of damage or accident. With a small apparatus, if any accident happens, and the lights go out, people are inconvenienced, and there is an end of it; but if the lights in Boston go out, that is a very serious matter. In the fifty years, nearly, of the existence of the Boston Gas Light Co., its lights never went out until the two nights after the great fire. In order to secure that result, of course the apparatus must be large, efficient, and well built, and that is an item of very considerable expense. With those works at the Island, as I understand, — I have never had the pleasure of seeing them, — they have this one item of the charge for coal, from which they get, either by meter or by measuring in their gas-holder, so many feet of gas. Of course it is very easily shown how much that gas costs per ton of coal. A ton of coal makes so many feet of gas, and the gas costs, of course, so much per thousand; no item, I believe, of purification enters into it, as I understand.

Q. If labor was added, 50 cents per thousand, it would make it cost less than $1.50?

A. It would cost more than 50 cents in proportion to ours.

Q. Adding the same cost for labor to the cost for coal, would not that make it less than $1.50?

A. Yes.

Q. Now, is there any gas company in the country that delivers its gas so cheaply and profitably, by reason of the location of the consumers, as your company?

A. Yes, sir; I mentioned the other day, when you asked me that question, that I thought the old New York company did; but I find that the Manhattan does, and the New York company does, and I think the Metropolitan. The Metropolitan company make more gas than we do, and I think it has about the same amount of distribution. There are three companies, at least, that are better situated than we are.

Q. You spoke about your iron retorts for your Albert coal; do you use them at all except for your Albert coal?

A. Yes, sir; we use them for the Albert coal in combination with other coals. The same condition of things, I found, existed for years at the Chartered Gas Co.'s works in London, and they were obliged to use iron retorts for the purpose of carbonizing the Torbane Hill coals.

Q. Upon your principle of allowing only one gas company to come into a large city, to supply the same district or territory, what inducement have you to make any progress in the art of manufacturing gas? You have got your consumers guaranteed to you; you have got competition kept off; what inducement have you to manufacture your gas more cheaply, so long as you have plenty of customers for your supply?

A. Precisely the inducement that every honorable

man conducts his business upon. So long as the Boston Gas Light Co. are the sole dispensers of gas in their district, it seems to me that they are honorably bound to make every exertion to manufacture the best possible article, and sell it at a fair price. Of course, the experience of every gas-engineer must bring before him all the new processes which are proposed for improving the grade and diminishing the cost of gas. It is as much for the interest of the Boston Gas Light Co. to discover some process by which their gas may be made for a less price, as it is for the consumers of the gas; because the cheaper we can make it, the cheaper we can sell it; and the cheaper we can sell it, the larger the consumption will be, and the more productive the property will be.

Q. Take, for illlustration, the telegraph companies. We all know the fact that the "Western Union" has been the principal telegraph company in the country; were you aware of the fact, that by the competition which has come in by the establishment of two rival companies, which are small in comparison, the "Franklin" and the "Pacific and Atlantic," the improvement in telegraphy has doubled, probably, within a few years, and that the expense of transmitting messages has been reduced about one half?

A. I was not aware that that was the cause of it; I know that influences have taken place which diminish the cost of telegraphing.

Q. You were speaking about Philadelphia. Is not Philadelphia extended over a very large territory, for its population?

A. It is.

Q. It is the most expensive city in the United States to supply with gas, because of its extent, is it not?

A. Yes, sir. I think it is sold at the outer parts at a little higher price than in the interior of Philadelphia. Supposing it were sold in all parts of the city at the same price, it is a very expensive city to supply.

Q. Is not the population more sparse in Philadelphia than

in Boston or New York; so that it costs more to distribute the gas?

A. I should say it was; Philadelphians would not tell you so, perhaps.

Q. You say no special expenses were included in your items?

A. No special expense in consequence of the fire.

Q. What did you have as a special expense in the year 1873?

A. We had the expense of relaying the burnt district with street-mains.

Q. Any others?

A. We had, of course, the purchase of a large number of meters for the new stores that were erected.

Q. I mean, throwing out the burnt district, did you build any gas-holders or do any work upon them?

A. Not to be charged to the gas at all.

Q. Did you build any?

A. In 1873, we did not.

Q. Did you do any thing at your works in Neponset?

A. We commenced our sea-wall in 1873.

Q. Did you make any purchases of land?

A. We made purchases of land in 1873.

Q. Did you pay for it then?

A. We paid for a portion of it in 1873.

Q. From what funds?

A. We borrowed the money.

Q. Do you remember how much?

A. I think we borrowed $100,000, and $100,000 was left in a mortgage upon the property.

Q. Then you say that, in your expenses for that year, there was nothing carried to what would be called construction account?

A. No, sir.

Q. There was nothing carried, as you would say, to the " plant "?

A. Nothing carried to the plant goes to the cost of the gas, and no interest on capital.

Q. Do you regard that as a fair average year?
A. Hardly, because we like to earn our dividends.
Q. I mean as to the cost of your gas?
A. Some years it has cost more, and some less. The cost of gas varies. depending very much upon the changes in different items. Of course the cost of labor and the cost of coal have varied, as gentlemen know, very largely, in the few years past, in consequence of the shifting nature of our currency all the time.
Q. You said that in that year you did not collect your bills at all from October first to November ninth?
A. In the burnt district.
Q That item went into the account of gas that you made, did it not?
A. That was in 1872.
Q. Then, in 1873, you had not that district to supply; you were without the opportunity of supplying that district?
A. No, sir; in 1873 we supplied it as far as it was ready.
Q. But you lost that portion of it which had not been rebuilt?
A. Yes, sir; entirely so. I ought to say, gentlemen of the Board, that, as you have heard, I have answered the questions that have been put to me; but if there are any questions on the part of the Board of Aldermen that they would like to put, of course I am here to answer, and shall be very happy to answer, both now and hereafter.

MR. MORSE. As far as the Boston Gas Light Co. are concerned, we will rest the matter here.

Mr. Field, for the Roxbury Gas Light Company, and Mr. Putnam for the South Boston Gas Light Company, also expressed themselves content to leave the matter as presented by the Boston Company.

MR. NEAL. The Charlestown Company does not exactly appear to oppose the petition; it appears somewhat as a friend of the court, to make statements, and see that no harm is done. The Charlestown Company is not at all alarmed by the state of things. We feel that, if gas can be made for a dollar or for fifty cents a thousand feet, by any new company, there is a very fine place to adopt those improvements.

Now that my brother Greenough has come out so handsomely, I am willing to "face the music," and give what our gas costs in Charlestown, where one of the Aldermen resides; and I hope he will continue to reside there another year. The net cost of our gas last year was 1.92\frac{6}{10}$ per thousand. I make the gross cost 2.21\frac{2}{10}$. We receive for coke, tar, rents, interest ("shop-earnings," as I call them) 28 cents, which leaves the net cost 1.92\frac{6}{10}$. Then the interest on the capital was 52$\frac{8}{10}$ cents, making $2.45. That is the whole story. I offer it without concealment. The price to the city is $2.50 for the street-lamps, and to the private consumer $3.00, with a discount of five per cent to large consumers.

While I am up, I would like to state that I have visited the Revere Sugar Refinery at East Cambridge, and got some new ideas about manufacturing gas by petroleum. I visited it in company with a gentleman who, I might say, is on the other side, but, at the same time, he is a very good friend of mine; and I found that the petroleum gas which is used is manufactured in an iron retort, with partitions; it passes through a washer and condenser into the gasholder, but no purifiers are required; then it passes into the building, and is there burned. But, if this petroleum gas was burned here as it is burned in the sugar-refinery, the difficulty would be, that the Board would be very likely to adjourn on account of the smoke. But they say in the refinery, that it does very well, because they are accustomed to smoke and smells. It makes a very beautiful light; but it is easily extinguished. A single wave of the hand, or a breath, almost, will extinguish it. I have talked with the gentleman who has that patent; and I can adapt it to the Charlestown Gas Works, as an enricher, perhaps to very good effect; but I am met with the threat that, if I do it, I am infringing a patent. I have no doubt that the gas is made for about what Mr. Nash has stated; but still it is not fit to be burned for general or public use. It requires some more thinning down. Then I would state that there is another process, the Gale & Rand process, in which these gentlemen are interested; and there is also the Olney process. I have seen those; and, if this opposition company is allowed a foothold here, the other companies can meet them with these other processes. The Olney process is used in the Harlem Works; and a sort of mongrel Olney process is used in the People's Works, Brooklyn; and it is used in the Citizens' Works; and the Gale & Rand process is used by the New-York Mutual Company. But I would like to ask, if gas can be made so cheap from petroleum or naphtha, why, in the name of suffering humanity represented by the gas consumers of New York, who are furnished with gas by the Harlem, the People's, the Citizens' and the Mutual Companies, they charge $2.75 per thousand? I know I am met by the statement of my brother Kennedy, that it is much better gas than is made by the Manhattan and Metropolitan Companies; but I think there is a difference of only two candles, from what I have seen. At the same time, I must admit that the Mutual Company furnishes very good gas. But the question is, Why do they charge $2.75 a thousand?

If there is any process by which the Charlestown Gas Co. can make gas cheaper than they do now, they will be very happy to find it out. Several processes have been proposed to me, as the agent of the company, which I am having under consideration. I am very desirous that some successful method should be found, by which gas can be made from naphtha, in combination, perhaps, with coal, so that the price of kerosene may be raised: because kerosene is a great competitor with gas, and we lose a great many customers by it; and in my travels round among the gas companies to procure statistics for Mr. Greenough, I found that there is a great loss of customers by the gas companies, on account of the cheapness of kerosene oil; and if we can, in a legitimate way, make petroleum or naphtha scarce, we shall be very happy to do it; and if we can at the same time reduce the cost of our gas, so that we can furnish it at $2.00 or $2.50, we shall be very happy to do it. But I must say that I am satisfied from all that I have learned, — and being not only the engineer of the Charlestown Gas Co., but acting as the financial officer of the company, I have taken pains not only to learn how gas can be made, but at what cost it can be made, and I have the cost of gas in many cases which I am not at liberty to make known, — I am satisfied, I say, from my inquiries and experience, that gas cannot be made from coal, in the city of Boston, and sold at a profit, for $2.00 a thousand. In theory it may be; but in practice I think it cannot. Still I may be mistaken.

MR. HYDE. I would like to ask a single question. What would the gentleman suggest in regard to raising the price of kerosene? Would it not be a good way to give one man the exclusive sale of it?

MR. NEAL. No, I do not think so.

MR. HYDE. You don't think that would effect it?

MR. NEAL. It might effect it. If I may be permitted to say a word or two on that point, it has been asked whether the competition in street-railways has not been a good thing; whether it does not bring down the prices. I have yet to learn that chartering the Highland Street Railway has brought down the price of tickets at all. I pay six cents for a ride, whether in the cars of the Metropolitan or Highland company, just as I always did. But that is not a parallel case. The Boston Gas Light Co. run their pipes in every street in Boston proper, and they furnish gas to all consumers. The horse-railroad corporation runs only in a few streets, comparatively speaking, and it seems to me that allowing another gas company to come in here would be just like allowing two or three horse-railroad companies to run over all the tracks of an existing horse-railroad company.

Mr. Hyde. We have no further testimony. We have some plans of the proposed works, which we will leave with the Board, without taking the time to exhibit them now.

The further hearing on the subject was then postponed to next Monday evening, with the understanding that the arguments would then be made.

ARGUMENTS.

ARGUMENTS.

MR. FIELD'S ARGUMENT.

W. A. FIELD appeared for the Roxbury Gas Light Company, and said : —

Mr. Chairman and Gentlemen : The Roxbury Gas Light Company was incorporated in 1852, for the old city of Roxbury, and now has capital stock to the amount of $600,000, and forty-eight miles of street mains, five miles of which have been laid through ledges : it has 4,200 customers, supplies 1,300 street lamps, and last year sold 77,000,000 feet of gas. The length of public and private streets in the territory is sixty miles. Speaking generally, it has about one-fourth the capital of the Boston Company, sells about one-eighth as much gas, lights about one-third as many street lamps, and has nearly one-half the length of mains, although not of the same size, in a territory the length of whose streets is about one-half the length of the streets in Boston proper. The soil of its district is peculiarly rocky and uneven ; a part of the territory is thickly peopled, and compactly built upon ; and part of it is thinly peopled, and has not yet lost all the characteristics of country.

This company has always felt bound to take the burdens as well as the benefits of its position ; has laid its mains through all the principal avenues of Roxbury, to the West Roxbury line, and has supplied the thinly-settled districts with gas as well as those thickly settled, and at the same price. Indeed, the only portion of the territory on which any money is made is the thickly-settled portions : the outskirts could not be supplied with gas at present prices without a loss. I think, Mr. Chairman and Gentlemen, any gas company which is permitted to supply gas through the streets to any city or district should be bound in a reasonable manner to take the burdens with the benefits, and has no right to confine itself to those parts of a district that are easiest of access, and afford the greatest profits. The very fact that a gas company is permitted to exercise certain public rights, i.e., that of using the public streets, imposes on it, to a reasonable extent, the public duty of supplying the whole district with gas. So far as I know, no well-grounded complaints have ever been made that the Roxbury Gas Light Company did not supply good gas at reasonable rates, and did not fairly and reasonably anticipate the wants of the city and its citizens in its district, or failed to do whatever it could be properly called upon to do, whether it would be for its pecuniary advantage or disadvantage. So much for this company.

In discussing the general subject, it seems to me that there are three questions involved : 1st, Are the citizens and the city supplied with good gas at reasonable rates ? and are they in all respects fairly treated by the gas company ? 2d, If at any time this Board shall be convinced that the citizens or city are not fairly treated, is the establishment of a competing company for the purpose of laying down pipes, and supplying gas in the same districts with the others, a proper remedy ? And, 3d, Has the petitioning company shown that it is able and willing to properly perform the functions it asks leave to assume ?

The first question, in a certain general sense, is the one that most concerns this Board, as representing the city and its citizens. I shall leave that to be discussed by the gentlemen who represent the other companies. I may, however, be permitted to say, that I think it has been conclusively shown by the evidence, that the city and its citizens are supplied with good gas at fair rates. Coming now to the two remaining questions, questions, too, which specially concern the case before the Board, I ask, Who are the petitioners ? and what do they want ?

The petitioners are a corporation established under the general laws, with a capital stock of $5,000. The existing laws permit them to increase the capital stock to $1,000,000, and no more. It is said, in evidence, that it is proposed to build works at a cost of $2,000,000, and to undertake to supply the most thickly-settled portions of the city with gas, at the rate of about one million feet a day, which is a little more than one-half of the supply of the Boston Gas Light Company. Something has been said to the effect that the petitioners have already obtained subscriptions to the amount of $1,000,000 ; but that seems to be unknown to some, at least, of the corporators. If there are any such subscriptions, they must be on a paper handed confidentially to the chairman of the Board, the contents of which I do not know; and if I did, I would not notice it, because, in public hearings before this Board, in my judgment, if I may be permitted to say so, no evidence should be admitted that is not publicly admitted, and no such thing as confidential evidence should be recognized. It is plain, then, that the present petitioners do not themselves intend to do any thing. They cannot go beyond $1,000,000 in their capital; and the least amount it is proposed to expend is $2,000,000 in works. The petitioning company, therefore, does not ask any thing for itself, any thing that it means now to use, any thing that it can now use, but says, if it can get the leave asked for, application will be made to the next Legislature for an increase of capital stock, or the incorporation of a new company, with sufficient capital stock; and it hopes that the leave here granted will enable it to get such legislation; and, if such legislation is obtained, it hopes to get subscriptions to the new stock to a sufficient amount; and, if such subscriptions are obtained, it hopes that the new company so to be organized will be able and willing to do what it now, although unable, asks permission to do. Whether any such legislation will be obtained, or any such subscriptions, is now utterly unknown; and the only use the petitioners can make, or propose to make, of what they now ask for, is to influence future legislation, and to transfer to some new corporation their rights. This is a very extraordinary proposition. Whether any company will ever exist that will or can act on the leave granted is entirely uncertain. The petitioners make many promises; but the body that is to keep them does not exist, and may never exist. Will it not be time enough to act on a petition of this character when there is any body before this Board, that has the legal capacity, and pecuniary ability, and actual disposition to act, and perform the functions which this Board is asked to grant? Again: what do the petitioners want? They say they want to lay down pipes now in the most thickly-settled portions of the city. They want the cream of the business: they will leave with the old companies the burden of supplying the more sparsely settled and less profitable parts. They will take only what pays best; and they want the right to select what pays best. In short, they want all of the benefits, and none of the burdens, and want to leave on the old companies all of the burdens, with as few of the benefits as possible. I need not say that this is something that has never been granted to any company, and would be, in any event, a most unjust discrimination, and one I am satisfied this Board will never sanction.

Look, now, at the second question: Is establishing a competing company a proper remedy for evils, if they exist? In the first place, I ask you to notice that the amount of capital invested in gas works bears a very different relation to the annual receipts from that in almost any other business. It is said that the capital stock of the Mutual Company is $5,000,000, and it sells annually 400,000,000 feet of gas. If that be so, eight per cent interest on the amount of the capital stock is one dollar on each thousand feet of gas sold. If the proposed company, on an expenditure of $2,000,000, can sell 300,000,000 feet of gas per year, there must be added to each 1,000 feet of gas sold, sixty-six and two-thirds cents to pay ten per cent on the cost of the works, to say nothing of the general expenses of management. Not only is the amount of capital required in its relation to the amount of business annually done enormous, but a large part of this capital is invested in property that has little or no value, except for the purpose of the manufacture and distribution of gas in the district in which the pipes are laid. Mr. Kennedy proposes to expend one of the two millions in putting down the mains in the streets, which is an investment of property that will be of little value, if they ever cease to be used for the distribution of gas.

Now, gentlemen, I hold it to be demonstrable, both from reason and experience, that competing gas companies in the same district are not only not a remedy for any thing, but are the worst forms, in every sense, in which any given population can be supplied with gas.

It is in evidence here, and undisputed, that the existing companies are able, and their works sufficient, to supply the whole city; and the companies are willing to do it.

It is evident, too, that any company that supplies gas must earn on its capital, in the long-run, a fair income. I shall not discuss with you what per cent is a fair income for gas companies; but whatever it may be, if, in the long-run, a company does not earn that, it will not do its business well: it will either stop business, or supply poor gas, and have poor works, and cease to anticipate the reasonable wants of the city and its citizens, and generally will fail to satisfy the public. You all know that it is only reasonably prosperous companies, that, in the long-run, do their business well.

Now every expenditure of money made by a competing company where the district is already well supplied is, economically considered, an unnecessary expenditure, and entails, unnecessarily, expenses upon the city and its citizens. If the proposed works are erected and carried on, the general expenses of the new company, and a fair percentage on its capital stock, must ultimately be paid by the citizens; and it is demonstrable, I think, that if new works of the same size and cost as the works of the Boston Gas Company are erected and used to supply one-half of the gas to Boston proper, distributed through all its streets, both companies, in order to live, must add from thirty to forty cents on each thousand feet sold beyond what is now added; and this the consumers must pay.

Again: the actual interference with the streets, which in any city is of great importance, and in Boston is peculiarly important, will be, by two competing companies, nearly doubled. You know all this a great deal better than anybody can tell you. Plans have been shown you of the sewers, water-pipes, and the horse-railroad-tracks in the principal streets, with all which you are very familiar.

The interference of the different systems of pipes with each other, the amount of the leakage, and the extent of the escape of gas into the sewers and water-pipes, will be increased. All this is so manifest, that it is enough merely to suggest it. But there is one other matter that may possibly have escaped your notice.

It is manifestly as important that a gas company should be directly and distinctly responsible for its neglects and torts, as a government should be for mal-administration. If there be two sets of pipes in the same street, it will not always be easy to determine where the fault lies, if there be something wrong with the gas. Take a leak in the streets in cold weather, the crust of the ground frozen, the gas coming out many feet from the actual leak. Neither company can know, except by digging, whether the defect is in its pipes or its neighbors'; and neither will be eager to remedy the negligence of the other. Now, because it is evident that competing companies necessarily increase the cost of gas, and the interference with the public streets, and the injury to the system of pipes and sewers laid in them, and diminish and divide the actual responsibility of the companies to a city and its citizens, all experience has shown that competing companies are an evil, and ought to be abolished where they exist.

In England and in Europe, — you have heard the evidence, — in all the large cities where competing companies once existed, they have been abolished, and, where more than one company now exists, they have been confined to separate districts. Wherever the people have, as has been stated, had much experience with competing companies, the evidence is, that they have been always abandoned. The people, then, prefer the consolidation of companies, and not the multiplication of them ; and in this country, where there have been competing companies, they have been abandoned, and each company confined to its own district. Indeed, the only instances of competing companies now existing that have been mentioned here are the Mutual Company of New York — which has existed a short time, I cannot undertake to say how long (it is said two or three years), and which has never paid a dividend, although it sells gas at $2.75 per thousand feet — and some companies in Detroit, which are also very recently established. It is said, that, in this country, no competing company ever paid a dividend. Whether that be so or not, this Board will not base any unusual action upon such recent experiments as the somewhat unsatisfactory examples in New York and Detroit. I need not suggest to you, that if two competing companies exist, whether they are run separately, or combine, the evils to the community remain, in great measure, the same. There is a double expenditure, a double interference with the streets; and the only relief that combination givesi s a single, instead of a divided responsibility. But it is said that a gas company is a monopoly, and competition is beneficial in all kinds of business. Now, Mr. Chairman, there never has been any objection to any man's making his own gas, or to any number of persons uniting together to make gas for themselves, provided their business affects only their own private rights. The petitioners do not need any license from this Board to do that sort of business. It is because they want certain public rights, i.e., to dig up the public streets and to lay pipes in them, and to use the pipes and the streets for distributing gas, that they come here at all. So far forth as your license is necessary for them, it is a license to do things that affect public rights and property. We all know that in large cities nearly everybody uses gas for light, and, in some respects, for heat, and that the lighting of the streets is the most efficient police ; and because all these things are in a degree for the common convenience of the inhabitants, and involve the use of the public streets, and interference with public property and public works, some have said that the gas should be manufactured and supplied by the city itself. That question is not before the Board. I only mention it in order to notice that it is precisely because of the *quasi* municipal functions that a gas company performs, that some persons contend that the city should make and distribute the gas. The argument in general, on the other side, is, that a city government, for various reasons, is not well adapted to carry on economically an extended manufacturing business like that of making and distributing gas; and that private enterprise can, if it chooses, do it cheaper and better; that it is in accordance with the principles of our government to leave to private enterprise whatever it can and will do well. But this question I am not here to discuss further than to say that these *quasi* municipal functions which a gas company must perform, to do its duty, and on which the advocates for the making of gas by the city rest their claim, show that the ordinary arguments against monopoly, and in favor of competition, do not apply to the manufacture and distribution of gas in cities. All government, within its limits, is a monopoly, necessarily so. This Board is a monopoly. The Water Board is a monopoly; the Superintendent of Streets and the Superintendent of Sewers are monopolies. If your superintendent of streets does not do his duty, you endeavor to make him; and, if you cannot, you turn him out, and make another man superintendent, who is also, while he holds the office, and within the limits of its duties, a monopoly. You would not think of appointing a second superintendent of streets to hold co-ordinate powers with the first, each with his committee employed in carrying out a separate street system throughout the city. You would not establish two water boards, each laying its pipes through the same streets. If you took the properties of the gas companies to-day, and undertook yourselves to make and supply gas to the city, you would not establish a double set of works to do one business. The truth is, that, so far as the streets are concerned, the only system you can ever adopt is that of one system of pipes for the same territory; and it is as unwise to permit competition in the supply of gas in the same streets, in the sense in which these petitioners use the word competition, as it is unwise to permit competition in the paving, in the sewers, or in the water works, of the city.

If a gas company, occupying a district, does not do its work well, it should be made to do its work well; and, if this cannot be done, it should be turned out, and some other gas company put in its place that will do the work well.

MR. PUTNAM'S ARGUMENT.

Mr. Chairman and Gentlemen, — The company I represent has probably little if any real interest in the result of this hearing, because it is not likely that the Citizens' Gas Light Company, if their petition is granted, will enter into competition with us. I hoped, at the beginning of the hearing, to obtain from them a disavowal of any wish to go outside of the city proper; but upon the question being put, whether they wished permission to lay their pipes in the suburbs, they said they wished liberty to go anywhere within the city limits, including West Roxbury and Brighton. We are therefore included in the petitioners' attack, and must make our defence. I shall, however, endeavor to be very brief, and to touch as little as possible on the general questions involved, as they have already been dealt with by Mr. Field, and will be gone over, doubtless, in still more detail, by Mr. Morse in his argument for the company principally concerned.

The South Boston Gas Light Company has a capital of $440,000, all paid in in cash at par. It has a little over twenty-one miles of street mains. It has two thousand consumers in a population of fifty thousand. It sells about 50,000,000 feet of gas, of which the city takes a little more than one-fifth for the street lamps. It sells about 115 feet of gas per annum for each dollar of capital stock. The Boston Company sells about three hundred feet per annum for each dollar of capital. It sells about one thousand feet in a year, per head of the population of its district. The Boston Company sells about four thousand feet per head. The dividends paid the stockholders have averaged, since the foundation of the company, seven and three-tenths per cent per annum on the capital stock actually paid in. For several years the company paid six per cent, then seven per cent, then eight per cent: during the war it paid six per cent only, then rose again to eight per cent, and for the last year only has paid ten per cent. This is all the stockholders have received from their investment; and I submit to you, gentlemen, as business-men, that their profits have not been excessive. They sell their gas at the same price as the Roxbury and Charlestown Companies, $3.00 per thousand; and I do not think you will find that gas is furnished more cheaply anywhere, where coal costs as much as here, and where the other conditions of prosperity are not more favorable.

It is easy to see why we cannot do so profitable a business, or sell gas as cheaply, as the Boston Company. We supply no theatres, no hotels, no City Hall, no dwellings of the very rich, where gas is burned extravagantly, and without regard to cost. Our gas is supplied almost exclusively to dwelling-houses, and to persons of moderate means and quiet habits, who burn gas with a wise economy, counting the cost, turning out superfluous burners, and keeping early hours. As you have seen, the population we supply burns only a quarter as much gas per head as the population supplied by the Boston Company. As the cost of distribution and of manufacturing plant is as great as if our customers took four times as much gas, it is obvious that we cannot make a profit upon our comparatively small sales without charging a higher price.

If it be said that the dividends we have made do not show our actual profits, and that large sums have been added annually out of earnings to the company's surplus, I can only reply, that I do not know how the fact is; but I hope it is true; for no well managed corporation divides its last dollar of earnings. It ought to have a margin to keep its work up to the increasing demands upon them, and to provide for unexpected contingencies, which are constantly liable to arise in a business involving so many risks as that of gas manufacture. But, if any surplus has been earned, it is all there. Not a dollar has been taken out by the stockholders in any form beyond the dividends I have named, and, whatever accumulations there are, the public are getting the benefit of without paying any interest on them whatever. The stockholders get only their dividend on the money they have paid in.

Now, the case of the petitioners is, *first*, that the companies are making exorbitant profits out of the supply of gas, and, *second*, that the way to cure the supposed evil is by introducing a competing company. I have dealt with the first branch of the case so far as it applies to the company I represent. I do not think the evil exists. But suppose it did to the fullest extent: the remedy proposed can by no possibility remove it, and is almost certain to aggravate it. I was somewhat surprised at first to see so many names of intelligent business-men among the petitioners for the new company; and happening, this morning, to meet a gentleman whose name headed one of the petitions, I said to him that I was rather surprised that he should have supposed he would get gas cheaper when there should be five or six millions of gas capital to pay interest on than now, when there are only two millions and a half. He said he hadn't thought of that; that he signed because they told him he would get his gas from the new company at $1.25 per thousand. I don't suppose any of the petitioners told that story; but

I fear some of the agents who circulate their subscription-papers are not as scrupulous as they should be. But the fact illustrates the easy good nature with which people sign petitions without inquiring as to their merits, and indicates how much value is to be attached to these supposed expressions of public opinion.

Nothing can be clearer than that the cost of gas to the entire community is measured by the amount of capital invested in the works, and the annual destruction of capital in the course of the manufacture and consumption of the gas. And, in the long-run, I believe it is equally clear that the cost of gas to the consumer will be in exact proportion to the amount of capital invested; so that by increasing the amount of capital, upon which interest must be paid, you necessarily increase the cost of gas to the consumer. Competition, then, by putting two capitals to do the work of one, works the very mischief it is introduced to cure.

George Stephenson, the first builder of railways, said long ago (and the saying has been quoted so often that it may almost be called an axiom of political economy), that, "when combination is possible, competition is impossible." The effects of railroad competition are familiar. We have lately had a very good example before our eyes in the case of two competing roads leading out of Boston, which have carried on a war of rates for some years back, doing each other immense injury; and finally, urged by everybody to combine, their customers and the public joining their stockholders in the pressure, wholly unmindful of the advantages of competition, they have at last ceased to compete, and are working in combination to the public advantage as well as their own. And yet competition is not nearly so objectionable in the case of railroads as in the case of gas companies. Railroads compete only at a few points; and we know that one of the chief complaints against the great through lines of railroad at the West is, that they charge enormous rates for local traffic where there is no competition, in order to make up the losses on business between competing points. Railroads, again, if business falls off in consequence of competition, can, to some extent, reduce the expenses of the business, and the amount of capital engaged in it, by selling off rolling stock, and diminishing the number and length of trains. And in almost every other employment of capital, when the business is diminished by competition, the capital invested can also be diminished. But a gas company's plant cannot be diminished. They cannot take up their mains. If they could, they would be worthless. Their capital is thoroughly locked up; their customers are limited to the residents on the line of their pipes; and whatever business a rival company takes from them can neither be replaced by new business, nor met by a reduction of their investment.

There is a competition between rival gas companies now going on in Detroit, which has reached an instructive phase. The old and new companies, in their competition for business, had reduced the price of gas to consumers to less than cost; and both companies were losing money very fast. The old company, however, has a good many customers outside the territory as yet occupied by the new one, which has naturally, as the petitioners propose to do, occupied the best territory first. It has now raised the price of its gas in non-competing streets to $3.00 per thousand. What the next move will be remains to be seen.

There are now in operation some very efficient checks against overcharging by the gas companies; and other remedies can easily be provided by legislation, if you become satisfied that an intolerable grievance exists that must be removed. Among the existing checks I will only refer to two. The first is the competition of kerosene and other oils. Where you want a room thoroughly illuminated, gas is probably cheaper than oil; but where you only want light enough for one or two persons to read, write, or sew by, kerosene will furnish it much cheaper than gas at any price at which it can possibly be afforded at present. In a population consisting mainly of people who count the cost of living, the competition of kerosene is very serious, as Mr. Neal has told you it is in Charlestown; and I don't think you will doubt his statement, that the gas companies would be very glad to find some way of cheapening their gas in order to meet this natural and inevitable competition.

The second is the force of public opinion, — a force not easily described or defined, but which is very distinctly felt. The company I represent has reduced the price of gas within the last four years, from $4.25 per thousand, which we were getting when we were only dividing six per cent, to $3.00 per thousand, the present price. And the other suburban companies have made a similar reduction. Now, either the gas companies must have conscientious scruples against making more than ten per cent on their capital, just as old-fashioned capitalists used to have against taking more than six per cent interest, or else they must have been influenced to this great reduction in price, by public opinion constantly pressing, in all its various forms, in one direction towards lower prices. You can ascribe their action to which motive you will. For my own part, I believe both motives had something to do with it. I believe — and I remember that Prof. Rogers, in the hearing before a committee of this Board some years ago, testified to the same belief as the result of his experience as State Inspector — that the gas companies mean to treat the community and their consumers fairly, and to furnish gas as cheaply as it can be done with reasonably prudent management of the property invested in the business.

If you ever become satisfied that the existing checks are insufficient, there are still two other methods of correcting the supposed evil.

In the first place, there is Mr. Nash's project, that the city should manufacture and distribute gas. This was discussed some years ago pretty fully; and, whenever it is brought forward, the gas company will probably be ready to discuss it again. Then there is the plan of regulation of the price of gas by an independent and impartial board of arbitrators, who should have power to examine the accounts of the gas companies, and decide upon their rates, with a restriction against reducing their rates below a point that would yield ten per cent dividend. Something like this is said to be the plan adopted in England, and now in force there.

CLOSING ARGUMENT FOR THE REMONSTRANTS.
BY R. M. MORSE, JUN., ESQ.

Mr. Chairman and Gentlemen, — I am unwilling to trespass upon your time after the remarks of my brothers who have preceded me; and I shall endeavor to confine myself to those considerations affecting the Boston Gas Light Company, which have not been presented in the other arguments.

I have to thank you, at the outset, for the very patient consideration you have given this subject during these somewhat protracted hearings; but I think you will agree with me, that the importance of the question has appeared more clearly as the investigation has proceeded.

You are called upon to determine whether the city shall reverse or change the established policy which it, in common with most other cities and towns in this country, has pursued in regard to the manufacture and distribution of gas. The claim of the petitioners is, that this policy is wrong, that a change should be made, and that that change should consist in opening the business to competition. The first consideration is as to the necessity for the change. In loose talk outside of this hall it is very common to assume that that necessity is shown. Without a patient, thorough investigation of the subject, without a knowledge of the considerations which should be borne in mind, citizens speak of the necessity for doing something in reference to the supply of gas, and seem to hesitate only as to the method to be adopted. I wish to call your attention mainly to the considerations which bear on this point. I shall undertake to show, from the trustworthy evidence that has been presented here, that that necessity does not exist; that the city of Boston is well served in the matter of gas, better served, in fact, than any other city in the country.

The real party in interest does not appear before you. That party is the gas-consumer. Petitions from large numbers of respectable citizens in aid of the petition of the Citizens' Gas Light Company have been laid before you; but remembering how easy it is to obtain signatures to petitions, and that no one is competent to pass upon a question of this kind, unless he has devoted himself to a study of details, you will attach no weight to the petitions of themselves. They furnish an additional argument for giving serious attention to the subject on your part, and that is all. As between the stockholders in the Boston Gas Light Company and in the proposed Citizens' Gas Light Company, you have no interest or concern. As representatives of the city, it is immaterial to you whether one citizen or the other invests his capital, and gets his return in this business. Other things being equal, you would probably say, that that company which has in fact established the business, and carried it on well, should be entitled to retain it rather than that the stockholders should be compelled to withdraw their capital from the investment so made, and new stockholders, in a new company, make investments to carry on the same business.

I will begin by assuming that there is no complaint against the general management of the Boston Gas Light Company: on the contrary, it must be conceded, it has been conceded, that it is managed in all respects, except as regards the cost of gas to the consumer, fairly and liberally. Mr. Greenough's testimony showed you that the company has made no charge for service-pipes or meters, and that it has made repairs in the houses of gas-consumers gratuitously, — a service not rendered by any other gas company in the world. Not only that, but men are kept in attendance, night and day, for the purpose of answering all complaints. The policy of the company has been liberal in anticipating the wants of the public as respects the laying of mains. In the entire term of the existence of the company, it has never had any controversy with the city in regard to the streets in which it should go, or the times when it should lay its pipes. It has, in fact, gone into new streets on the application of a few consumers, whose business would be entirely inadequate to pay the expenses of laying the pipes, trusting to future business to pay for the investments. At a hearing which took place several years ago before a committee of the city government, opportunity was given to all citizens having complaints to make against the management of the company to appear, and state the grounds of those complaints; and, in answer to that advertisement, no parties appeared; and we may assume that there is the same absence of complaints now, inasmuch as evidence of such complaints would have been the most obvious and material evidence to have been laid before you in support of the claims of these petitioners.

Again: no complaint is made as to the quality of the gas furnished by the Boston Gas Light Company. It is admitted to be at least equal to the best that is made: it may fairly be claimed to be superior to any other. It is in evidence that the coal used in the manufacture is of the most expensive kind, — more expensive than that used by any other company, — and that the average illuminating power is from eighteen to nineteen candles. Nor is it contended that the company has shown any disinclination to answer proper inquiries as to the conduct of its business. It is not to be expected that it should be ready to gratify the curiosity of everybody applying either at the office, or through the method of a public hearing; but it has always evinced a disposition to meet the proper authorities of the city in the manner in which any person or corporation charged with the performance of a great public trust should meet those who have imposed the duty and obligation upon them. The company have regarded this as an important, sacred trust. They have considered, that, in discharging it, they owed fidelity to the public as well as to their stockholders; and they contend that the management of their affairs, in all the respects to which I have referred, has been honest, fair, and liberal.

The only ground of complaint is as to the cost of the gas to the consumer. This is, of course, of main importance. If it can be demonstrated that as good gas can be made and furnished at a less price than by the Boston Gas Light Company, it is conceded that some new instrumentality must be established to do it. But this is a matter to be shown by proper evidence, and not to be assumed without thought. I do not mean to apply any technical rules of evidence; but I ask you to determine this question upon a fair consideration of the same points as would enter into your decision upon any of your practical business questions. It must be remembered that the petitioners have sought to establish this point in regard to the high price of the gas furnished by this company; it must be assumed that they have exhausted all available means to place that testimony before you; and, if they have failed to to do it, it must be assumed that that evidence does not exist.

The testimony on this point comes from different sources. First, from the prices as established in other cities. The price of gas in New York is $2.75 per thousand feet; in Baltimore, $2.75; in Chicago $3.00; in St. Louis, $3.09; in Brooklyn $2.75 to 3.00; in Washington, $3.00, — though I believe, since the publication of the pamphlet to which I have referred, the price there has been reduced to $2.50. In New York, Brooklyn, Baltimore, and Washington, the price of coal is much less than it is in Boston. In New York, there is competition in a part of the city. Mr. Greenough was asked whether there were not greater facilities in Boston for the cheap distribution of gas than in any other city; to which he replied that three of the New York companies, to wit, the New York Gas Light Company, the Manhattan, and the Metropolitan, had better facilities than the Boston Gas Light Company. In Philadelphia, the price is $2.30 per thousand feet, but the price of coal and labor is very much less there than here. Relatively to the cost of those articles, the price is greater in Philadelphia than in Boston. The price in Detroit is manifestly not a proper standard of comparison. The testimony is that the companies there are not receiving, at the present rates, one-half the cost. This, clearly, is only a temporary price, which neither company can possibly maintain for any great length of time. It is only a question of endurance. One company will buy the other out, they will divide the city into districts, or they will agree as to the price to be charged. In any case the price will be much higher than it is now.

The result of all the inquiries into the prices in other cities is that, having regard to the cost of the materials that enter into the manufacture and distribution, as well as to the quality, of the gas, the price of gas is lower in Boston than in any other city in the United States. This I believe to be the general opinion outside of Boston. One thing is certain : that, if the citizens of Boston have just ground of complaint in regard to an excessive charge for gas, the citizens of the other cities I have named have much stronger ground of complaint.

It will be said, however, that all gas companies charge an excessive price, and that this review simply shows that the Boston Gas Light Company, is less exorbitant than companies in other cities. I proceed, therefore, to consider the next class of evidence.

I refer, secondly, to the testimony as to the actual cost of gas. Mr. Greenough testifies that in 1873 the Boston Gas Company received, for all gas sold, $2.39 per thousand feet. That is to say, the retail price is $2.50, to wholesale consumers there is a discount of five per cent, and the street lamps are supplied at $2.08 per thousand. The receipts, therefore, average $2.39 per thousand feet. The actual cost of making and distributing this gas was $2.08. To this is to be added an allowance of two per cent for bad debts, and we have 2.12\frac{1}{2}$ as the actual cost of the gas. Deduct this amount from the amount received, and there is left an actual profit of twenty-six and one-half cents per thousand feet. Twenty-six and one-half cents per thousand upon 612,-000,000 feet sold during the year is less than ten per cent on the capital as it stood last year, two millions of dollars. In this statement of cost, Mr. Greenough has allowed nothing for street mains, or for labor in laying the pipes; nothing for meters, of which a very large number had to be furnished last year in consequence of the fire, and nothing for interest on the capital. It may be said that last year was an exceptional year, and that the cost will be less this year. Mr. Greenough has testified that that cannot be ascertained until the accounts are made up. When they are made up, he will be able to state whether or not the company can reduce the price of gas. So, too, it may be said, that, whatever may have been the result of the business of last year, larger profits must have been realized formerly. I submit that that is wholly immaterial to this inquiry. If larger profits have been realized, only ten per cent, by way of dividends, has been paid to the stockholders. Any surplus received by the company has gone into property now owned by the company, from which the consumers derive benefit, without being called upon to pay interest upon the additional capital which might otherwise have increased the capital stock. It is of no importance whether, at any time in former years, the price might or might not have been fixed at a lower rate than that which was maintained. You are to deal with the matter as it is presented to-day. If you believe this statement to be true, and there is no suggestion that it is not true, you cannot find that the price charged was unreasonable in view of the cost to the company.

Again: in Charlestown, Mr. Neal testifies that the actual cost last year was 1.92\frac{6}{10}$ per thousand feet; but the gas is of poorer quality than that made in Boston, which will account for the difference in the cost. The price in Charlestown is $3.00, however, as against $2.50 in Boston. In Jamaica Plain, Mr. Pratt testified that the actual cost last year was $3.00; and that when the city was proposing to contract with them for supplying the street lamps, and offered to pay $2.75, they stated that they would prefer not to sell any gas to the city than to furnish it at that price; and that, if the city were not satisfied with the price of $3.00, the books of the company would be open to the inspection of the city officials, upon the city agreeing to pay whatever, on an examination of those books, appeared to have been the actual cost to the company. Perhaps the latter portion of this statement was not embraced in the testimony of Mr. Pratt as given to you; but the fact is within the knowledge of members of your Board, who were upon the committee dealing with this subject.

As against this testimony as to the actual cost of gas in Boston and vicinity last year, Mr. Nash testifies that the gas made at the Revere Sugar Refinery in East Cambridge, in which he is interested, costs, he thinks, not more than seventy-five cents per thousand feet. But this gas is made not from coal, but from petroleum; and the evidence has shown you that gas can be made from petroleum much more cheaply than from coal. As to the quality of the gas, it is proper to remind you that Mr. Neal testifies that he has been out to examine it, and that he does not think it a gas which would be regarded as satisfactory by you. It burns with a beautiful flame, but can be easily put out, as by the wave of the hand. At the same time, Mr. Neal thinks favorably of the idea of making gas from petroleum, and is desirous that this and all other processes should be fairly tested. Mr. Baldwin, whom we all know as one of the Directors of Public Institutions, says that the gas made at the House of Correction and at Deer Island costs $1.05 per thousand feet; but Mr. Greenough has pointed out in his evidence that this estimate includes only the cost of the gas at the mouth of the retort; in other words, the cost of the coal alone. There is no allowance for labor, as that is furnished mainly by the inmates of the institutions; there is, of course, no expense of distribution, and an absence of many of the items which enter into the cost of a large company supplying a city. In fact, these last two instances are not at all in point in determining the cost of the manufacture and distribution to a great company undertaking to supply a large community. There must be costly apparatus; there must be a sufficient reserve to enable the company to meet all emergencies; there must be large expenses for labor, — none of which are included in the cost of supplying a single building or a small group of buildings.

The remarkable feature of this part of the case is, that the petitioners have not brought here one man engaged in the manufacture of gas from coal, to supply a town or city, to testify as to the actual cost of gas. They rest their case entirely on the opinion of Mr. Kennedy, that it can be made for a dollar and a half per thousand feet, and sold at a fair profit for two dollars per thousand feet, — these prices being based upon an estimated consumption of three hundred million feet during the year As they have seen fit to rest their case mainly upon his evidence, it is necessary to consider what weight should be given to it; and, as a preliminary, to inquire what are his interests in this matter, what have been his antecedents, how largely is he entitled to the confidence of this Board? I say nothing against Mr. Kennedy personally. I have no doubt he is a man of property, of large experience in the construction of gas works, and a man who intends to state facts and opinions honestly. But he has a large interest at stake here. He expects to build the works for this new company; he expects to have the substantial control over the disposition of two millions of dollars. He is advising a company of men utterly without knowledge on this subject, who are trusting to his judgment and advice. When a young man asks an older one to lend him capital to set up in business, or to join him as partner, he is likely to take the most sanguine and hopeful view of the situation. It is not to be expected that Mr. Kennedy would present any thing but the most flattering side as well to his stockholders as to the public. He is to own two thousand shares in this company, — a much larger amount, I assume, than that owned or controlled by any other individual. Whatever the result of the business, his profit will be very large in the building of the works, the laying of the pipes, and the beginning of the enterprise. Again: it is fair to call your attention to the history of the company with which he has been identified, — the New-York Mutual. That company, which is now competing with an older company for the supply of gas in New York, has a nominal capital stock of five millions of dollars, although in fact only one-half that amount has been paid in. They are making gas from naphtha, at a cost of less than $1.50 per thousand feet, and selling it at $2.75 per thousand feet, supplying 400,000,000 feet during the year; yet they have never paid a dividend. One thing or the other is certain: either

Mr. Kennedy is grossly mistaken in regard to the cost of their gas, or else the company is managed in a very different manner from the management we expect from any honest and well-organized company. Again: it is worthy of remark, that this gentleman, who proposes to make three hundred million feet of gas, at a cost of $1.50 per thousand feet, and supply it at two dollars, is making in New York four hundred million feet, at a cost of less than a dollar and a half per thousand feet, and supplying it at $2.75. There is nothing, therefore, in the relation of Mr. Kennedy to this enterprise, or in his antecedents with the New-York Mutual Company, which entitles his opinion to great weight before you.

But, in addition, I call your attention to Mr. Greenough's comments upon Mr. Kennedy's estimates. Mr. Kennedy stated that upon the sale of three hundred million feet of gas, at two dollars per thousand feet, the cost of which was one dollar and a half per thousand feet, a fair profit could be realized upon a capital of two millions of dollars. We know from the testimony of Mr. Baldwin and others, that these gentlemen would not consider any thing less than ten per cent a fair profit; yet fifty cents a thousand, upon three hundred million feet, is less than ten per cent upon two millions of dollars. Moreover, Mr. Kennedy calls the cost of coal in his estimate, 72 cents per thousand feet, as against 87 cents, shown by Mr. Greenough to have been the cost to the Boston Company. He allows for labor 25 cents in place of 50, shown by Mr. Greenough to have been the actual cost.

Upon a fair review of Mr. Kennedy's evidence, taken in connection with the other testimony before you, it is certainly not proved that the present price is excessive. On the other hand, it is undoubtedly true, that new processes may be invented, or that other substances than coal may be found to yield equally good gas, and that they can be stored and handled with safety; and, in either case, the existing companies are in a condition to avail themselves at once of the improvements, and have every disposition, as most certainly it is for their interest, to adopt them. The cheaper the price, the greater the sale, and the larger the profits. The nearer the price of gas can be reduced to that of kerosene, the more gas will be sold, and the more money made by the companies. And I desire to say that I am authorized by the Boston Gas Light Company, and the other companies within the city limits, to request the Mayor and Aldermen to appoint a commission of competent and scientific engineers, whose duty it shall be to investigate the various processes for the manufacture of gas from petroleum and kindred substances, with the understanding that the entire cost of the investigation shall be paid by the companies. We hope in this way to settle the question one way or the other, at least for some time to come. On the one hand, if new processes can safely and profitably be used, the companies will unquestionably adopt them, and thereby a reduction in price may be obtained. On the other hand, if the processes are found to be without merit, the result of the investigation will remove one cause of complaint against the present companies. Mr. Greenough has told you that as yet he has not been disposed to adopt any of the methods for making coal from naphtha. He does not believe that you would consent to the storage of so large a quantity as would be required in their business.

These remarks cover all I desire to say upon the question of price. I shall pass very briefly over the remaining questions, as they have been fully discussed before you.

Assuming that you are satisfied that a change in the method of supplying gas is required, I still submit that competition is a fallacious and expensive remedy. The capital at present invested in the gas business within the limits of the city is about five millions of dollars. The actual value of the property owned by the companies, and used in the business, is in excess of that sum. This capital is sufficient to supply the present needs of the city. Pipes are laid wherever they are needed. The apparatus is in all respects ample and suitable. The profits from this business enable the companies to pay dividends varying from eight to ten per cent. Is it conceivable that consumers will get their gas cheaper by the city permitting two millions of dollars of additional capital to be invested in the same business? On this point, I can add nothing to the weighty words of John Stuart Mill, which were read in your hearing by Mr. Nash. When sufficient capital is employed to do a certain business, an increase of the capital must result in an increased cost of the products of the business. A certain, though perhaps not immediate, result of the permission to a new company to maintain its works, and lay down its pipes, will be to increase the price of gas. Upon this subject, we have not merely the opinions of sound and thoughtful men : we have the actual experience of other cities before us. In London, there has been competition to the extent of at least four competing companies in some parts of the city ; but the city is now divided into districts, each company occupying a single district. In Paris, there was competition, which proved such a nuisance that the Emperor was obliged to consolidate all of the companies into one company, which has a monopoly in the entire city. In New York and Brooklyn, the price remains the same as before competition was tried. There is not an instance where the price has been permanently reduced by competition. At the same time, in passing, I may remark by way of encouragement to parties intending to invest in the new company, that there is not an instance on record where a competing gas company has paid a dividend. When, therefore, the petitioners say, "Why not let us, if we are willing to do it, risk our money in trying the experiment? We do not ask the city for the money: we ask only to risk our own," — the answer is, "We have no concern in your risking your money, of itself; but we cannot agree to it, because thereby we help to impose a debt on the city and the citizens, which they must ultimately pay."

The practical inconveniences arising from the excavation of the streets for the purpose of laying pipes for the new company have been already sufficiently commented upon. I believe that if these alone were fairly presented to the respectable citizens whose names are upon the petitions brought in here, they would be sufficient, in their judgment, to outweigh the apparent advantages to be gained from competition. Who is to pay for the disturbance and blockade of the streets, for the accidents which may occur in the progress of the works, for the injury to the pavements and to the existing pipes? And who can calculate the confusion and the differences that will be likely to arise between two gas companies hereafter, each with sets of pipes in our narrow streets?

Even if the petitioners were fully organized, with a paid-up capital of two millions of dollars, it would be a serious matter to grant this petition. I have endeavored to show why, even then, it should be refused. Yet you are asked to grant this privilege to a company with a capital of five thousand dollars, which proposes, if you grant the permission, to increase it to a million; which then proposes to petition the Legislature for leave to increase its capital to two millions of dollars; which then proposes to raise the two millions; and which, at the end of that time, may be under the control of an entirely different set of stockholders and officers from those who now manage it. I venture to say, that no application of this kind was ever made before, and certainly no such application was ever granted. If any corporation is entitled to the great privileges which this petition seeks to obtain from you, if at any time the city should deem it wise to permit competition in the supply of gas by granting permission to another corporation to lay down its pipes, that corporation should be fully organized, with a capital sufficient in amount for its business, before it seeks such a privilege at your hands.

With these considerations, I submit the matter to your judgment.

MR. HYDE'S ARGUMENT.

[In consequence of Mr. Hyde's absence from the city, he has not been able to write out his argument; and the following abstract from the "Evening Transcript" is therefore all that can now be given. The argument in full will be inserted in the second edition of this volume.]

Mr. Hyde said the question was not a new one. Again and again has the investigation of gas been discussed; but, whenever they go to the city of Boston or to the Legislature, they are met by an array of gas companies opposing the desire of the people to rid themselves of a monopoly. He had sat for twenty-three nights as a member of the city government, trying to get information as to the cost of gas; but they were defiantly told they should not have it. While the investigations are in progress, they are supplied with good gas. It always has been so; and gentlemen had told him they hoped this investigation would keep on, for they get good gas: it doesn't sputter, and one can read by it. There are six gas companies in this city; and is there a gentleman in the city government who would want to buy them out at their own figures? It is apparent to every one, that, when stock cannot be bought in the market, there is no loss in making gas. They will not reduce their price until compelled to do so by competition: they will not even adopt means of cheapening gas, or use the improved appliances for manufacturing it. He believed that the day will come when the streets of Boston will be lighted by gas made from petroleum for one dollar; but this cannot be done under the present system. Until competition entered into telegraphy, one message only could be sent over one wire: now two messages can be sent over each wire in each direction, making four in all. There is nothing so odious to the people as a monopoly; and here is a monopoly in one of the necessities of life. Here are these companies fighting inspection, giving up here a little, and there a little, but as closely fighting it to-day as ever. Here are these gentlemen who ask the privilege of manufacturing gas with their own money, and offer to sell it at less than the present price; and they are supported by nine thousand citizens, whose streets are to be dug up. He believed the citizens should have the privilege of choosing between two companies in purchasing a necessity of life. The remonstrants were afraid that the petitioners would carry out their plan: the petitioners would give a bond to any amount that they are acting in good faith. His belief was, that the petitioners would do what is proposed, and do it quickly. There is a corporation in our midst with a paid-in capital of $2,500,000, and property worth $8,000,000; and the time will come when the stock must be watered to $8,000,000. Mr. Morse interrupted Mr. Hyde, and said the property was worth only $3,500,-000; and Mr. Hyde asked if they would sell for that; which Mr. Morse said he was not authorized to answer. Mr. Hyde said the new company would be compelled to go into whatever streets the citizens should demand; and, if the company did not submit, the people could go to the Legislature, and get a law compelling it. The gas companies had fought every thing but the proposition to allow them to continue to carry on a monopoly. Mr. Hyde contended that abuses exist; the streets are not to be opened until after due consideration; and, in conclusion, he urged that the Board decide this question before they go out of office, and protested against the reference of the subject to the next city government, but desired the giving of that disposal to the subject which is best for the interests of Boston.

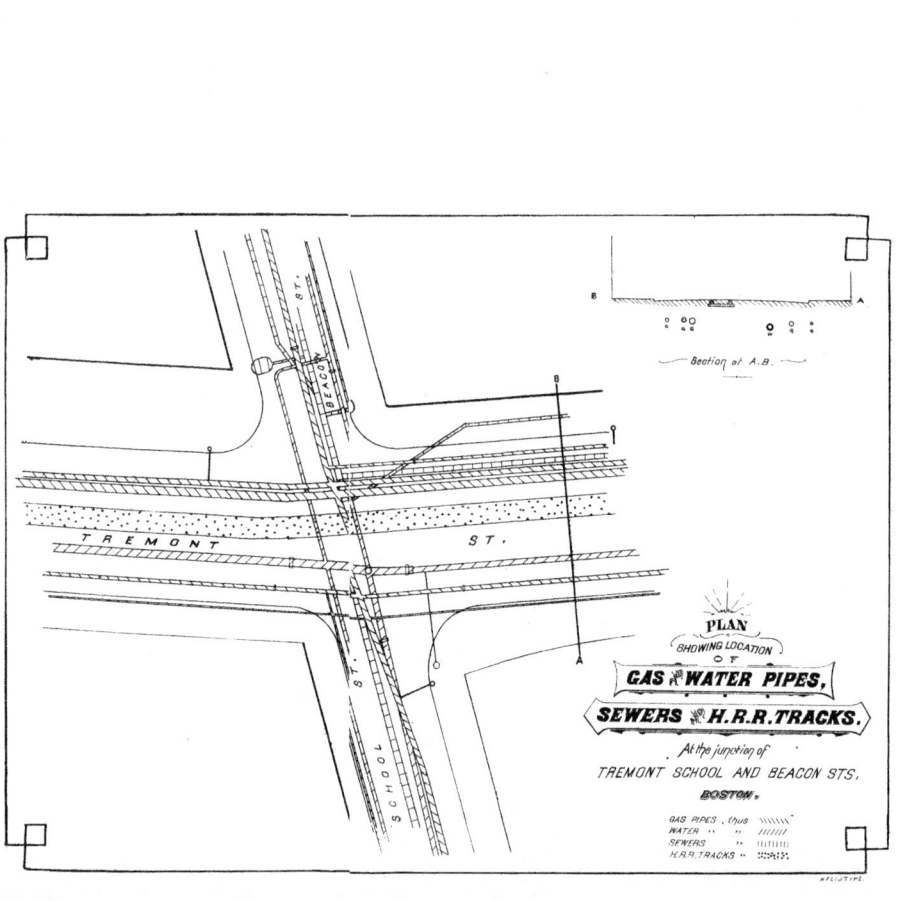

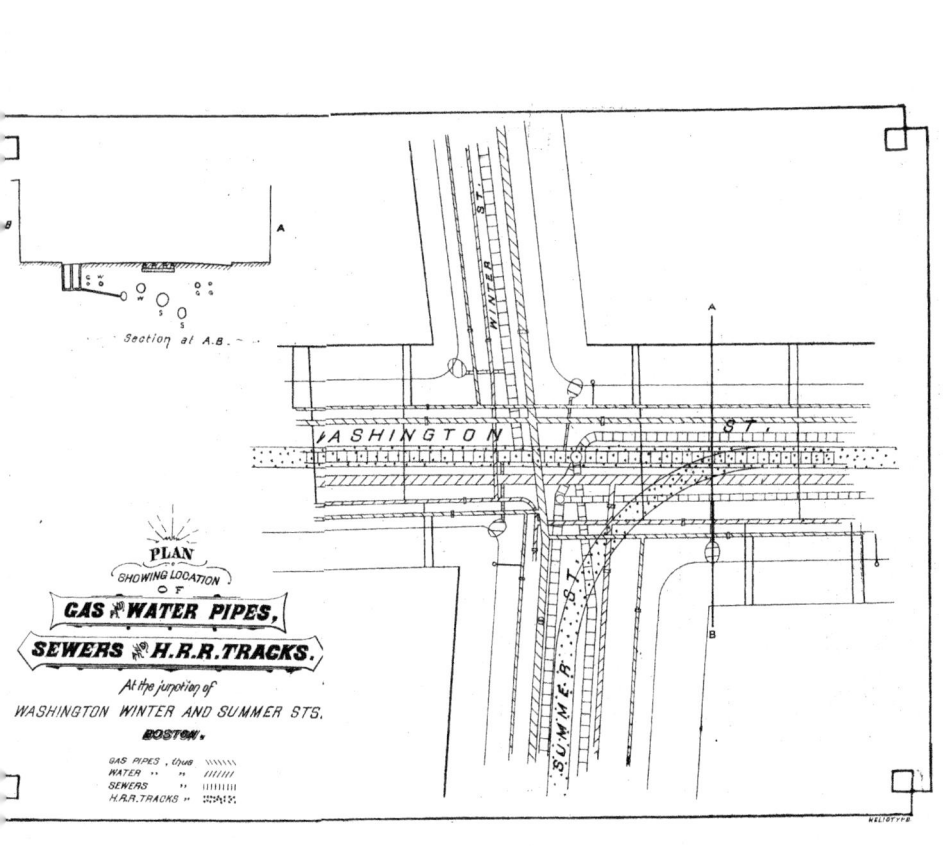

Printed in Dunstable, United Kingdom